"YOU'RE SO TALENTED"

(CONFESSIONS OF A WORKER B)

Barbara Klar

Epigraph Books
Rhinebeck, New York

"You're So Talented": Confessions of a Worker B Copyright © 2024 by Barbara Klar

All rights reserved. No part of this book may be used or reproduced in any manner without consent of the author except for in critical articles or reviews. Contact the publisher for information.

Paperback ISBN 978-1-960090-72-0
eBook ISBN 978-1-960090-73-7

Contact the publisher for Library of Congress Control Number.

Book design by Colin Rolfe

Epigraph Books
22 East Market Street, Suite 304
Rhinebeck, New York 12572
(845) 876-4861
epigraphps.com

I'm lucky to have met Barbara Klar in my life. Enjoy her story." —GAIL BARACANO, Former Art Teacher in NYC Public Schools

"Wearing Barbara Klar's jewelry on stage empowers me to do my best. I have been a fan of Barbara's Clear Metals collection since she opened her first store in 1984." —STEVE JORDAN, rock and jazz drummer, American musical director, producer, songwriter, and musician. Currently, he is the drummer for The Rolling Stones. During the 1970s and 1980s, he was a member of the bands for the television shows Saturday Night Live and Late Night with David Letterman

"Barbara Klar is one tough cookie. But when you are unconventional, original, independent, as driven as you are consummate, and a woman, you sure as hell better be. In telling her story, notable names and influential people come in and out her life, engaging her, romancing her, challenging her, supporting and disappointing her, but their input never diminishes your awareness that this gifted artist never compromises her mission or passion to create jewelry that is more than uniquely beautiful. Barbara's work is an extension of her relentless curiosity and most importantly, her belief that each of her strong, sensual and hypnotic pieces will help you express the power that each of us possess. This is the tale of a benevolent sorceress, and I'm so happy to have been bewitched by her for so long." —HAL RUBENSTEIN, former fashion director and founding editor of *InStyle Magazine*. Former men's style editor of *The New York Times Magazine*, Rubenstein also created and edited the cult classic *Egg Magazine*. Rubenstein is the author of *100 Unforgettables Dresses* (Harper Design, 2011) and *Paisley Goes With Nothing: A Man's Guide to Style* (Doubleday, 1995). Most recently he is the author of *Dressing the Part: Television's Most Stylish Shows*. A native New Yorker, he has no desire to live anywhere else.

PRAISE FOR "YOU'RE SO TALENTED"

"Barbara Klar's story of her life and her art—her life within her art—is a tale of highs and lows and lifelong learning. We are crushed along with her when she sees her work undervalued, demeaned, stolen, copied—but we rise with her when she creates. While she has achieved full mastery, she is constantly evolving and expanding, and she makes the experience of inspiration and execution palpable even if we've never looked through a jeweler's loupe." —LUCY SANTE: Writer, Collage Artist, and Photographical historian. She is is a Belgian-born American writer, critic, and artist. She is a frequent contributor to *The New York Review of Books*. Her books include *Low Life: Lures and Snares of Old New York* (1991), and, more recently, *I Heard Her Call My Name*

"This is a work of love forged by defiance. This book is a testament of Klar's bold journey, of her Ohioan beginnings: father, mother, last child and shadows the intimacy that allowed her to forge a life of an artist in ruthless Manhattan. Her mother's mysticism was a gift of independence. Her father's meticulous mind inspired wonder at the mystery of the magical locks and levers that hook us into our fleeting beauty on this earth. Klar creates works of art to work in our bodies, allowing metals and gems to become the encasement for our immortality. Her exquisite and bold reliquaries hold love to preserve beauty beyond decay; they soar with belief and hope. My Chinese ancestors believed jade protects our mortal bodies for eternity. Klar's creations are powerful symbols of life and vitality. Her book is a testament of her devotion: pure as a monk's, clear as rain, and eternal like pine." —FAE MYENNE NG, American novelist and short story writer. She is a first-generation Chinese American and recently was awarded the winner of the California Book awards for non-fiction with her book, *Orphan Bachelors*

"When I'm with Barbara, I feel both immediately at home and yet completely captivated by what I learn from her stories, her craft, and her generous soul. All of that shines through in you're so talented, which is part hard-core punk rock gumption and part touchy-feely love poem to her art. Not only does do her tales from the glamorous grungy corners of nyc remind me of all the fun that i had back in those days, Barbara's stories also serve as reminders that with passion comes the ability, the permission, to do anything! Brava, Barbara!" —ABBE ARONSON, writer and the grande dame of PR, marketing, media, event planning and "artful schmoozing" in the Hudson Valley. She is also the author of the blog, "What's Shove Got to do with It?" and a contributor to Jenny online magazine

"As I approach my 78th year, I take pause and reflect on the past. Growing up in New York City in the 1950s was quite remarkable. Oftenmy mother and I would to walk downtown to the East and West village along 8th St. We would visit the lovely jewelry and craft shops. To name a few, Sam Kramer, Phyllis Jacobs, Bill Tendler, and Art Smith would sell copper jewelry on the side walk. I fell in love with handmade jewelry at 8 to 10 years old. After college I became an art teacher in a public JHS in Fort green Brooklyn. Spike Lee was in my first class when he was 12 and I was 21. At Art school in New Paltz I met my husband and we began a long 50 year plus marriage. My husband was an art and rare book collector. We would spend our weekends in bookshops and as he spent hours perusing them, I searched out jewelry stores. One lucky day we walked into Clear Metals, Barbara Klar's small East Village store on 7th St where she lived and worked out of her studio. On weekends, she would open her the small front of her studio as a store. I was completely blown away by her fabulous necklaces, rings, bracelets and earrings. Her jewelry reminded me of the 50s jewelry I loved, and her craftsmanship was excellent. It reminded me of the famous silversmith George Jensen. Sometimes later we met. Barbara and bonded instantly. I'm thrilled by her friendship and we have been friends for over 30 years. Over the years I have collected such wonderful pieces. When my husband passed away three years ago Barbara made me an amazing book Locket which I will always treasure.

[CONTENTS]

	Introduction	ix
1	When Creativity Opened My World	1
2	The Fascination with Craft	5
3	Introvert or Extrovert	7
4	The Fondue Set	11
5	Job Hunting	23
6	Tiffany's	40
7	Artwear, 1981	48
8	7th Street	51
9	The Story of the Aegis	60
10	Symbols	65
11	Moving the Store to SoHo	68
12	The Clients	73
13	Copyright and Infrinegment	78
14	Leaving NYC	82
15	What Cancer Brought Me	85
16	Living to Create	92
17	The Journey of the Balangandan Necklace	99
18	Why I Make Reliquaries & Memento Mori	112
19	Doubt (Epilogue)	126
	Acknowledgments	129

Barbara Klar, 2015 photo by Franco Vogt

Introduction

It goes like this: If I had a quarter for every time I heard this in my life, I'd be a wealthy woman. When I moved to NYC from Cleveland in 1979, I was fresh out of art school, completely unprepared and naïve. I pounded the pavement with my portfolio under my arm and looked for work in my craft. Eventually I started a business and now I say "Talent" is only 5% of what it takes to be successful, let alone be happy.

In writing this book I try to address the dreams and desires of young people who want to go their own way. Creatives, like me, that jumped off that cliff with only their passion and dreams as their parachute: Talented youngsters who have no guidance or support systems in place to fuel their journey. I had no business training in art school and the things I learned along my path had big implications in the decisions I made. Many of my creations have stories that accompany their development. I want to provide this book as a companion piece to the legacy of my work that will carry on beyond my life span.

I have made my living as a jewelry designer and metalsmith since 1984. Early on, I supported myself as an office temp worker and worked nights on my jewelry until I found a small jewelry studio/school where I could work. In the school, I cleaned the studio in exchange for free bench time. Eventually, I had two sequential stores in NYC where I did custom, wholesale, and retail jewelry. I worked with famous designers and showbiz personalities. I consider myself to be one of a handful of women in a male dominated industry. When I walked into an interview with Cartier's, all I could see were rows of benches with men doing the work. In 1980 when I got a job in the Diamond District of NYC, all the men in the room would hold my mistakes up in the air and talk and laugh about me in a foreign language. That's when I chose to go my own way and fall back on my office skills to support my jewelry habit. To me, jewelry is art, and it is so personal because one puts this art on their body and in doing so, transforms the meaning into a personal talisman. It becomes a spiritual act of art, and I could only do it with my own love behind the process.

It wasn't until recently that I realized my path as a metalsmith and jeweler from NYC's lower east side to Woodstock, NY was a journey that was part of a long tradition. Jewelers Sam Kramer, Art Smith and Winifred Mason had stores and studios in the 1950's on 8th St. My store was on 7th St. and like Art Smith, part of my joy has been to make jewelry for performers. In 2018 I repaired a grand necklace created by painter Rolph Scarlett.

Rolph lost the support of patrons when his style changed, and he retired to Woodstock where he lived in "regional obscurity" to the end of his life. He also returned to his original passion of making jewelry.

The last 15 years of my creative life I have continued to make my living through jewelry, yet I have created pieces in secret that are objets d'art. Objects that one could wear yet have meaning on their own such as the Faberge pieces that the house created for the Romanovs. Some reflect the lifetime spiritual quest we all consider, and some reflect the struggle of women's work. These final works are the culmination of my lifelong journey which have led me to my definition of success. Success is not what I imagined it to be in 1979.

[1] When Creativity Opened My World

In the beginning I learned to hide. I learned to observe, to watch. I preferred my dark green corduroy overalls to the pink taffeta dresses that resembled wedding cake frosting. I preferred collecting worms in the rain and placing them in my overall pockets and watching my mother scream when she did the laundry. She'd reach her hand into the pocket and shout in disgust. I developed my sense of humor by working with my father in his workshop. I loved the engineering challenges we faced together in the basement. When we solved a challenging problem, he would say to me: "Why, you're so smart, Barbie, why aren't you President?" This never ceased to amuse me, and I grew to naively believe that being President was a sincere possibility.

We both learned to hide from my mother. She was fighting her own demons and could be unpredictably rageful. I was the youngest in this family of five with a brother and a sister who had left the house by the time I was five. I was the good girl, in my room. I loved my tiny crank Singer Sewing machine and taught myself to make clothing for my dolls. My father had built a large drawer, desk and cabinet section in my room where one part had louvered doors with a long shelf. Here I would arrange my prized "Dream Kitchen" that was complete with small samples of canned food, roasted turkeys, and table settings. I had a full Barbie Doll family. Alone in my room, I amused myself endlessly while the scent of roses in bloom would blow through the translucent ruffled curtains my mother had sewn. Eventually she would open the door without knocking and demand I go outside and play.

Dream Kitchen (above)

I still prefer the magic of working alone in my studio where I still love tiny things. When I investigate the depths of a precious stone, I see the gardens my parents toiled over. I see my mother's multicolored gladiola flowers swaying in the breeze of a summer's afternoon. In the sky I see the ocean I didn't see in Ohio. I smell the roses.

The tools in my father's basement workshop were lined and organized to convenient perfection. Nails and screws were kept on shelves in labeled jars. My most joyful memories were with my father on his trips to the hardware store. These stores had more shelves with more parts than were in his workshop. While he was shopping, I would stand alone in the aisles and study the hinges and locks.

How did they lock and how were they put together? I'd fold them over in my hands and try to reverse engineer them. One time my father decided to build a Mystery Box for my nephews when they were very small. He painted it silver and installed hidden compartments with bits of hardware complete with sliding door bolts and chains. It was fascinating to watch my nephews discover how these things worked and opened. The process of building this box intrigued me.

When I was older and we moved from the country into a small town, I was still working in the basement. Only now I was working at the sewing machine my mother had just bought from Sears. It smelled of oil and hummed like a cat's silky purr. It had a bar by my leg that, when pressed, would lift the foot off the fabric and away from the needle. I'm not sure where my mother had learned to sew, but I now suspect that she learned at the elbow of her mother as a child when they both were servants in the "Rubber City" mansions of Akron as Hungarian immigrants. This is where she probably developed her sense of style, beauty and flower arranging. She knew how to do so many things, but I was never told how she learned them because the history of my family was rarely discussed. I remember how she used to love to dress us in matching outfits she would sew and assemble with impeccable detail. The sewing machine had embroidery settings and I would sit at her side listening to the whir of the needle as it laboriously sewed tiny interlocking hearts onto fine wool. We would go to fabric stores and examine the draping and texture of every bolt of fabric until we had matched it to the McCall's pattern she was going to make.

Years later, when I was 16 and sitting alone in the basement at this same sewing machine, I was making elaborate carpet bags like the ones I saw on Peggy Lipton and Janis Joplin. I was visiting the coffee shops around the Kent State campus and trying to absorb the hippie vibe. My carpetbags had hidden pockets and zippers. They were made of cut velvet upholstery material, lined in satin, and embellished with satin curtain cording. They were big, slouchy, and glamorous. I was so proud to rock them with my bell-bottoms, espadrilles, and tube top!

Cleveland wasn't that far away, so as soon as I could drive, I started going to the Cleveland Muscum. I would sit on the benches in the huge rooms with arched ceilings and stare at the Dutch Masters and Pre-Raphaelite paintings. I'd step closer and study the details of the brush strokes and clothing. I'd especially study the jewelry in the paintings. It was here where I first noticed that many of the ladies were wearing "top knuckle" pinky rings. I immediately went home and searched for my sister's old baby ring I knew was buried in my mother's jewelry box. My mother wouldn't let me claim it, but by the time she said no I had found an old gold-fill ruby baby ring in an antique store. It fit perfectly on my left pinky finger just below my top knuckle. I did not know then that this would become my personal secret goldsmithing symbol and extend to my other fingers.

In a new town with few friends, I continued my quest for creativity. I took high school art classes. I opted out of college prep and gym class. Later I found this had a huge impact on my college exams and flunked them horribly. Thank God that my mother had insisted I become part of the Business Office Education program when she emphasized that I should never rely on any man to support me. I should make my own way. My 120 wpm typing skills were to come in handy when I moved to NYC and had to support my art habit.

[2] The Fascination with Craft

A reformed Catholic, my mother discovered Unity when I was five. Unity is a religion based in metaphysics and it was housed in an old mansion. Unity had bought a huge Tudor Home and Coach house from one of the rubber magnates when Akron was experiencing a deep decline, and the suburbs were booming. Unity was primarily an adult congregation of misfits and mystics. Void of other children, I would roam this mansion unsupervised. I would run my hands over the weathered mahogany bannisters and the brass hinges as I searched for ghosts in the fur closets. I discovered two wall safes and learned to hear the clicking of the gears as I put my ear to the metal and tried to crack them open. There were dumb waiters and secret staircases. The bathrooms were enormous and stunning with glistening tiles and vintage porcelain. There were carvings in stone with brass hardware that adorned the fine cabinetry. In the basement there was a second kitchen used for events with the original stoves and sinks. Down a few steps was a larger room that had been used as a small theatre with a rotating stage. There was a fourth-floor ballroom full of gabled windows with nooks where a small child could curl reading a book. A butler's quarters next to the ballroom had the smell of dried flowers and incense. Amber lighting illuminated this mysterious library with carved mahogany woodwork.

As I roamed these hallways with fascination, I imagined the workers who created this masterpiece of architecture and design. Who were they? Where were they? How did they make this?

Not only did my curiosity become inspired, but I learned to

meditate. Unity installed a bio feedback machine where we learned to take power of the mind over the body. We studied the Bible yet not in a literal way. At 7 years old I was smacked in the face on the playground by another child when I announced, "Jesus was not real". I had learned that he was only written to convey "the ideal human" in a book of inspirational fiction.

I am expanding here because I want to emphasize how important it is to follow the signs on a path. The journey is the meaning. I may have developed a love of craft in this mansion, but it was my ability to learn to control my mind through meditation that stabilized me on the journey for which I was never fully prepared. My journey forward resembled falling off a cliff without a parachute. As a child I had nightly dreams of falling over a cliff as it wrenched me from the depths of sleep into a panicked, sweaty fear. I learned to combat this when I trained myself to imagine myself gently falling into a pile of hay when I fell off that cliff in my twilight travels. The dreams stopped. Fear, however, did not.

[3] Introvert or Extrovert

Building a private world in the louvered closet with my Dream Kitchen and Barbies and working with my father in his basement workshop did not prepare me for the world. It taught me that I was safer in my own world than I was out there. I was terrified of a nuclear war when we were shuffled weekly into the shadowed halls located in the subterranean school passageways in first grade. We were instructed to crouch under the desks and cross our hands over the back of our heads.

We did not live far from Dayton Ohio where Wright-Patterson Airforce Base was located. When my parents and I would go to the movies, my mother could be seen whispering quietly with the dark-haired owner in a corner of the cavernous theater before and after the movie. I would pretend I was going to the bathroom and try to listen covertly to their conversation by the water fountain. I heard them whisper of captured UFO's which were allegedly stored at Wright-Patterson. I became increasingly disturbed, and my nightmares amplified. My mother would come into my bedroom at night, and we would meditate about tomorrow's math test. Together we would visualize my success at passing these exams, but eventually she noticed my anxiety about the bombs and the aliens. This is when she told me that if there was a nuclear war, not to look for her or my father. Just go with the aliens who would arrive in their enormous spaceships to save a percentage of the population, of which I would certainly be one. From that moment on I would walk the woods behind our house and look for evidence of alien visitation. I looked for Fairy Rings too. I kept my head up and looked at the sky obsessively. I saw what I took to be a silver spaceship when I was a child on the school playground in second grade. I watched as it moved silently in its silver majesty, gleaming in the sunlight. And then it was gone. I started believing they could save me from this ridiculous life on planet Earth.

I wanted to leave.

Later, in 3rd grade, my class took a trip to "Serpent Mound" in Ohio. This is a large mound that retains an abundance of mystery around it's time of creation. Who made it, was it the Indians? Why was it shaped like a snake? Did it contain buried treasure? It was huge and long, covered in luxurious green grass, and raised above ground level about 4 feet. My classmates and I climbed over it and wondered aloud about its origin. I was equally curious about the symbol of the snake. What did it mean or represent?

By the age of 11, I was a regular at the library, delving into books about Native Americans and UFO's. I discovered paranormal books about Ghosts and Poltergeists and became fascinated with otherworldly concepts. I was a believer.

When Apollo 11 first landed on the moon in 1969, my mother and I sat anxiously in front of the TV. I had such awe for the bravery of these men. I had respect in the knowledge that something was out there so big it was beyond my comprehension. That's when I started watching any movie, old or new, that had to do with outer space. There was Flash Gorden and Lost in Space. Later there was Star Trek and Star Wars. The original 1951 movie, "The Day The Earth Stood Still" is my favorite movie to this day.

When my mother took me to see a replica of the Rosetta Stone, I discovered hieroglyphs and symbols that could represent words and language. I did a deep dive into Ancient Egyptian history. Today I am obsessed with the Knight Templars.

I was not only obsessed with what may be out there, but with the designs of the future: the clothing, the communication devices, the portals which led to other worlds. When my parents declined to take me to the 1964 World's Fair in NYC I was devastated, since I could imagine nothing more thrilling than this vision of the future now.

In my present, there was nothing more interesting than the past or the future. The past and the future were rich with undiscovered secrets. I feared and dreaded my present as I became an awkward adolescent with few friends. When I was in high school and studying business office education, I forced myself to conquer my fear of being seen and took a drama class. I remember sitting in the front row of my first class with my palms sweating and my stomach aching. I watched in awe when a tall and lanky young man stood to speak in the front of the room. He was confident, humble, and funny. He was wearing a striped boat-neck French T-Shirt, "La marinière". Even though he was not traditionally handsome, there was something about him with his prematurely grey hair, long expressive fingers, and full lips that I found achingly intriguing. He was odd and brilliant, and his name was Jim Jarmusch. During class we became friends and eventually began a relationship. My first love. There was nothing Jim could not do. He could illustrate hilarious comics, write for the school newspaper, or take amazing photos. He was an avid music fan and opened my sheltered world into an avalanche of possibilities. I will never forget meeting his parents. Jim's mother, Betty, was a writer with the most beautiful pageboy of white hair I had ever seen. His father was a lawyer who was gruff and humorous with a very heavy air of intimidation. Yet what I most remember was their colonial house tucked into the woods full of dark wood and oriental rugs. When I would visit, Jim's mother would excitedly show me the most recent antique her mother, Gammy, had found at the flea market.

Our (open) relationship lasted 10 years and he was the impetus on my moving to NYC in 1979. In my mind I thought that we now would have the opportunity to live together and be a couple. He was going to NYU Film School, and I had just graduated from the Cleveland Institute of Art. While that did not happen, we remain friends to this day, and he has been with a very talented and wonderful film director ever since. This is my chosen family.

Fondue Set: 1979, Cleveland Institute of Art,
Raised, Carved, Fabricated, Cast, Forged
Silver, Brazilian Rosewood

[4] The Fondue Set

> "Yes, an oil slick on the Cuyahoga River - polluted from decades of industrial waste - caught fire on a Sunday morning in June 1969 near the Republic Steel mill, causing about $100,000 worth of damage to two railroad bridges. Initially, the fire drew little attention, either locally or nationally."

It had become the studio joke during my years of study at the Cleveland Institute of Art that I was going to throw my Fondue Set in the river. The Cuyahoga River had gained some notoriety when it caught fire in 1969 and was forever immortalized by Randy Newman in 1972 when he recorded his song, "Burn On". Everyone in Ohio knew that song and thought The Cuyahoga River was a sad homage to life in Cleveland.

Working on this Fondue Set for three years had become my tale. Perhaps I was the joke because my instructors never took me seriously. Or ANY of the women in the Silversmithing Department in this small "Ivy League" art school of the Midwest. Eventually, I heard whispers that the women were just going to get married, so why should they be given the magical information regarding metallurgy?

Nothing deterred me then. The mind-blowing concept that by wielding hammers, stakes, and a blowtorch I could craft a hollow form from a flat piece of silver should not be something I was afraid to do. I should have known better.

Always the rebel, I was NOT going to follow tradition. At night, in the hushed space of the departmental offices, I roamed and researched what the previous graduates had made for their thesis. I opened their thesis books and saw only traditional tea sets. No, really? They all looked alike with their carved ebony handles and customary finials and spouts. No, I wouldn't make a Tea Set. I would make a Fondue Set even though I'd never eaten fondue in my life.

Fred Miller and John Paul Miller had formed the CIA Metalsmithing Department in the 50's. They claimed to have re-discovered the ancient art of granulation. They were influenced greatly by the emergence of Danish Design in the 1950s and 60s. They wore lab coats when they taught and there were rarely any women in the classrooms. I never considered that I could be excluded from their history and knowledge based on my sex.

At CIA, the first two years of the 5-year program were basic skills and art history training. One didn't even choose a major until the third year. Even though I'd spent two years studying art at the University of Akron, I had to apply for advanced placement at CIA after one year of work with an art review by the instructors. It wasn't an easy or friendly environment. However, if one played their cards right and kept a 3.8 grade average, a student was eligible for the traveling "Gund Award" which was a $10K traveling scholarship upon graduation.

The key to this Gund Award was work and then more work. I kept my head down and that's what I did: work. I noticed there were favorite students in the department, all males. I chose my bench space next to one of the favorites and watched him from the corner of my eye. I studied his tools from afar. He had obviously been doing this metalsmithing gig a lot longer than I had because he had a large and beautiful crafted antique oak tool chest with his initials gold leafed onto the top.

There were, for the first time in history, 6 women in the Metalsmithing Department in 1974. We developed a kind of intimidated and fearful camaraderie when we noticed the men filing into the glass-walled inner office sanctum. Behind closed doors, they talked with

THE FONDUE SET

the instructor, all nodding heads and inside joking. Left alone together in the studio, my fellow females and I locked eyes. The men filed out of the office, and we returned to the banging of hammers against polished steel stakes and the humming of the polishing machines.

With a bowed head, I hammered the bowl of my fondue set intently. Slowly and steadily my instructor walked towards me as the men filed out of the office. He removed the bowl from my hands and held it eye level, speaking loudly to alert the class to attention. While I had been excluded from obvious inside information, I was chastised for doing it the wrong way. I was made an example. Humiliated, I left class and returned to my apartment. My anger formed a palpable cloud above my head. It didn't matter that a week later the bowl fell from my tongs on its way to the quenching bath and I caught it in my left hand, so it didn't fall on the floor thereby potentially ruining weeks of work. Only I noticed the smell of burning flesh that permeated the room.

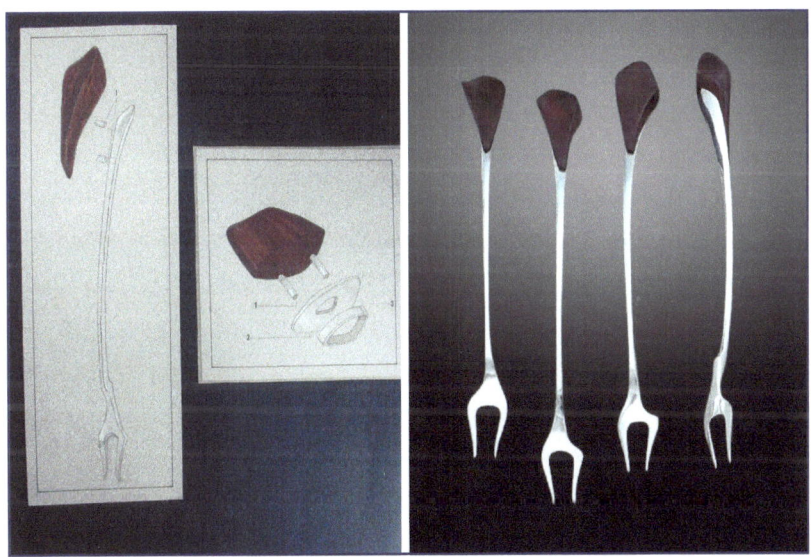

Forged and Carved Fondue Forks
Exploded view drawings of Handles and Forks

The stream of financial reward through juried competitions, big and small, fueled distrust among us. It appeared there was an unspoken requirement to not only diligently follow design tradition but also research an individualized well-developed path. We guarded our designs with subversive secrecy, rarely sharing technical information or design inspirations. It seemed that only men won the scholarships and challenges. That's when I began to spend a lot of time at the Cleveland Museum of Art, which was conveniently located across the street from the institute.

The Hall of Armor was my favorite. Its vaulted ceilings were hand-painted to resemble a 15th-century castle. The lifesize horse mannequins wore armor, and I feasted my eyes upon the etched steel and polished rivets. The swords and shields were beautiful and ominous. I roamed through the museum until I found cases of small objects that had originally been housed in churches. I discovered momento mori and reliquaries that held pieces of bones as jewels. Reliquaries became my obsession and creative passion. When I made my own reliquaries, I felt like a scribe working on a sacred transcript under a tent in Egypt.

Covertly, I made reliquaries. In the evening within the metal studios, I made a box that was turned in cherry wood on a lathe. It had an enameled circle around its top, which represented the journey I made through the rolling hills of my mind. There was a silver hinge and a clasp. I set a garnet upside down, point facing up to the heavens inside a silver "capstone". On the inside, I placed a small drawing with the hair of my beloved encircled by a silver wire coil. My art and my love become my wink at the reliquary because what we considered precious and vital was truly subjective.

I kept working on the Fondue Set. Raising the bowl of the pot, raising the small alcohol lamp, each had mechanisms that fit together with handmade screws, tension fit lids and a carved, silver-lined, rosewood base. Time-consuming and challenging, this work grabbed me with a perverse obstinacy I aimed toward completion: The light at the end of

My first reliquary, 1976
Walnut. Glass Enamel, Silver, Garnet, hair from my beloved and drawing on the inside. "Art" is the reliquary of importance held within

the tunnel. In-between this stubborn project, my dreams were filled with reliquaries and what they meant to me and whether or not there was a God.

My secret piece de resistance was The Triptych. I studied Dante's Inferno. I had my own youthful inferno welling inside and I had my friend Charlie as my secret weapon. He was my roommate and friend and I considered him a genius and true renaissance man. He knew before I did that art school was a waste of time. Before he dropped out, I remember that he disappeared for a week into the woods outside of

Cleveland only to reappear with an address to his mysterious location in preview of a big reveal for his last sculpture class.

One Saturday morning in spring we drove to this location. I sat in the front seat of my car, stunned at the mass of two large trees balancing a rock and a piece of steel as it swayed gently in the breeze. His sculpture was about 20 feet tall, and he'd done this alone in a field. It seemed to me that he had just built his own pyramid in a field in Cleveland.

I wanted to make my Triptych about my own personal earth, heaven, and hell. I made a collage with pencil and watercolor. I made silver reticulated hinges and a locking mechanism. Charlie made a beautiful walnut box in three parts complete with pointed arcs and an inset window for a dried rose petal with the hair of my beloved, Jim. He steamed and bent the walnut to form the arc at the top of the 3-part case in the bathroom of our apartment. This was one of my best attempts at collaboration and a testament to the labor of love and friendship. Neither of us wanted credit, we merely wanted to create.

The Triptych took about 4 months to make. Upon completion, I quietly opened it up and stood it in a corner of the metals studio during a group critique. I had a lump in my throat as I held my breath. In a room of over 20 student objects, it was the largest piece and the only piece that received no criticism, positive or negative. It was silently overlooked and unacknowledged. Once the critique was over, I wrapped it in brown velvet and replaced it in the handmade foam core box Charlie had made for it.

THE FONDUE SET

17

"YOU'RE SO TALENTED"

Triptych Reliquary, made in Collaboration with Charlie Spademan, 1977 Walnut, watercolor, collage, Sterling Silver, Hair, Thread (@23 inches tall X 16 inches wide when closed)

Crushed and deflated, I realized I would have to go outside the boundaries of my own department to know if I'd made something good or bad, interesting, or boring. I approached the lone female design teacher who taught at CIA and arranged a private critique with her. She was the only streetlight in a dark corridor and didn't understand why I felt so despondent about the Triptych. She told me it was masterful.

The Fondue set was heading towards completion when I entered the Triptych in another educational scholarship competition. I didn't win this one either, but another male student did, and I was furious. My grades, I felt, were being sliced in half regularly even though my work was good and my attendance flawless. I did more than required but my grades did not permit me the earned challenge of competing for the Gund Award, the graduating $10K traveling scholarship. That's when I approached the woman who was the Dean of Students.

Speaking my mind was never easy for me. I felt that another woman would surely understand my frustration and step up and speak on my behalf. Later that week I learned that my instructor had been awarded a grant for a reliquary he'd just made which he had submitted into a competition in Cleveland. It was accepted into the Museum Show. I had been working on my reliquaries at night, often when he made an appearance. Imagine my amazement when my grades improved overnight, and this instructor told me that I always had to do things the "hard way".

That's when I internally gave up. I gave up thinking I was not good enough or worthy of the Gund Award. No longer eligible, I started working on things I only wanted to make and stopped keeping backbreaking hours in the studio. I spent my nights listening to rock concerts at the Pirate's Cove or The Agora in the flats of Cleveland. I saw David Bowie, Iggy Pop, the Runaways and Devo. I was happier. My Fondue Set Thesis and The Triptych made a proud appearance at my finale critique. To my shock and amazement, it was widely attended with students and teachers outside of my department and I even got a round of applause.

The year after I graduated, I heard from a fellow female student that she'd won several competitions and received some scholarship money. Two years later I realized that my educational experiences may have not given me any business training but had perfectly prepared me for my next creative journey: New York City. (If you can make it there, you can make it anywhere!)

My comment on the whole process, 1978

[5] Job Hunting

In 1979 I was packing up the Uhaul in the driveway of my childhood home and preparing to move to NYC fresh from art school in Cleveland. My mother whispered in my ear and said, "It's okay, I know you'll be living out of a sink for a while." I had no idea what she meant until I found myself renting an unfinished loft on West 36th St with my friend Cynthia. The raw space had one small green porcelain sink in a bathroom with open slats for walls. That sink was the only source for the washing of dishes and me. Now I finally understood what she meant as I tried to make sense of a space that was not a home.

I thought I had an extensive portfolio that proved my talent. 36th street was within walking distance of the Diamond District in Manhattan. Before my move, I had calmed my anxiety and fear by browsing the NY Times Help Wanted Classified Ads. Repeatedly, there were over 5 pages of ads looking for jewelers. "I could get work", I told myself.

Clutching my portfolio under my arm and tucking a few prized pieces of my jewelry creations in my bag, I walked from my loft on West 36th St. dodging pushcarts and garmento racks of clothes draped under plastic. The sidewalks were bustling with activity as I smelled the creativity wafting through the industrial buildings with their tall windows angled out for ventilation. I heard the sewing machines humming and the taxi horn's taut impatience in the congested streets. There were no earbuds for me to wear in 1979 to dull the sound. I felt the butterflies of anticipation walking to my interviews in the Diamond District on 45th St. until a stray male hand touched my breast or cupped my rear end. Often, I would feel the warm breath of an unshaven chin on my neck as words like "Puta" and "Nice" pierced my air of confidence that swirled around me like a humid summer breeze. By the time I had reached the Diamond District for my interview I was deflated and fearful, but I'd put on my invisible armor and pretend I was fine.

I had never seen jewelry sweatshops like these before. Typically, they were several floors up in tall, non-descript buildings on W. 45th street and were accessible by small, unstable elevators. Once inside I'd wait in a double-locked entryway and be interrogated in a narrow foyer between two locked doors as I was inspected through a camera I saw high in one corner. Once inside, I'd meet with the foreman in the tiny workroom with side-to-side, row-to-row workbenches. Heads were bowed in concentration. I saw rows of torches spewing soft flames at every elbow. The foreman would look at my portfolio and up at me, wordlessly, repeatedly. There were no women in these rooms, only men. They typically spoke little or no English.

The first time I was hired to work in one of these small rooms I was paid minimum wage and challenged by the other workers to exhibit my skills. I had never worked in a manufacturing environment, and I had never used a high temperature mini torch. I had little experience working in gold. When I would melt the tiny gold prongs on the setting of a ring, I would first hear the gasps and then the stifled chuckles ricocheting around the small room like a game of telephone.

They put my bench next to the only stone setter, Juliano. He was a man in his late thirties, and he traveled from shop to shop, setting stones on a freelance basis. He dressed in pressed white shirts that were open at the neck to reveal layered gold chains. His black pants with creases and his shiny black shoes lent an air of professionalism to his dapper persona. When I was mocked, he was the one who gave me support without a glance sideways. "Turn down the oxygen, more gas", he would say softly. I liked Juliano even though he wore too much cologne. When his hand started to touch my hair or linger on my thigh,

I became nauseous. At first, I thought it was his cologne, but I soon realized that these men in this room made for a toxic experience that was impacted by my daily walk to work. It was all too much so I quit.

Next up, I had a job interview at Cartier. The workshop at Cartier on 57th St. was on the top floor above the store. It was huge, full of rows and rows of workbenches. When I visited and met the shop foreman, they were all dressed in lab coats in the whispering silence of thick concentration. Once again, I saw no women in the room aside from the receptionist outside the glassed walls. The foreman, Benson, was a fatherly gentleman in his mid-fifties. I noticed how clean and well-manicured Benson's hands were and I wondered silently if he ever got his hands dirty in this workshop. I nodded as he asked if I'd be willing to work 40-hour work weeks with an additional 20 hours regular overtime at minimum wage. Benson looked at my portfolio and asked me if I would take a lie detector test. I hadn't expected this, but I said yes, I had no problem doing that. The next day, as I was wired to a monitor in front of a man I had never seen before, I wondered why this was happening. What could I possibly have to hide that might be perceived as a threat in taking this job? Question upon question I answered with little fear. "Have you ever stolen anything?". "No, only by mistake when I walked out of Ben Franklins with a pack of Neccos still in my hand. Immediately I went back in and paid for it." "Do you take drugs?" "Not really, but I smoke pot." The interview ended and I waited a week for a phone call that never came. Finally, I put a call into Cartier and asked to speak to Benson. "Have you made any decisions on the job?" I asked quietly. "Yes" he said. "Am I still in the running?" "No", Benson replied. "You failed the lie detector test because of the question pertaining to drugs. "Oh, but I only smoke pot, doesn't everybody?" Benson was not amused. Looking back, I find this hilariously audacious.

Some pieces that were in my portfolio when I was job hunting and pounding the pavement in NYC:

Fibula, 1977, Inlay, bronze, silver gold, wood, fabricated.

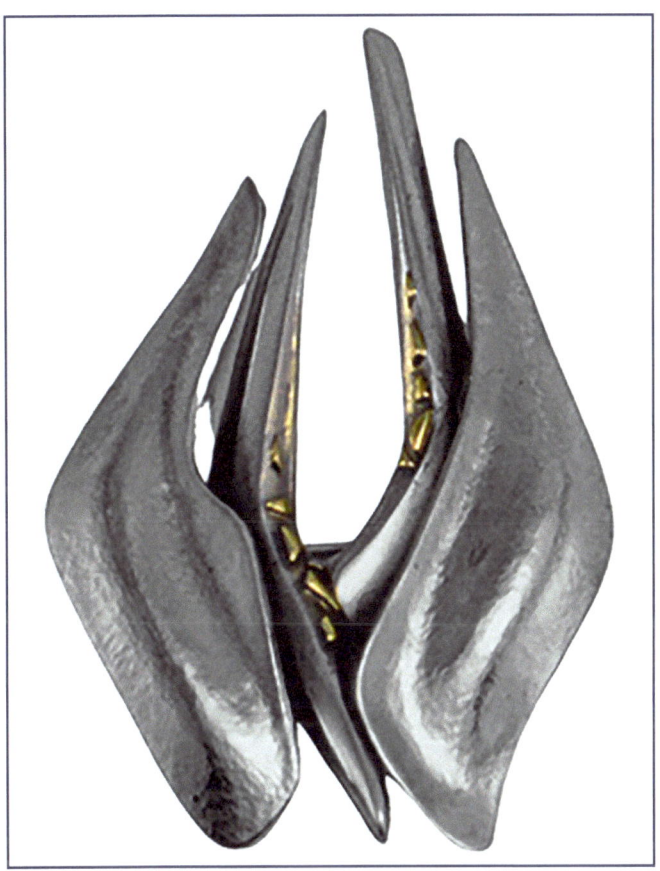

Repousse Pin, 1977, silver and gold, fabricated

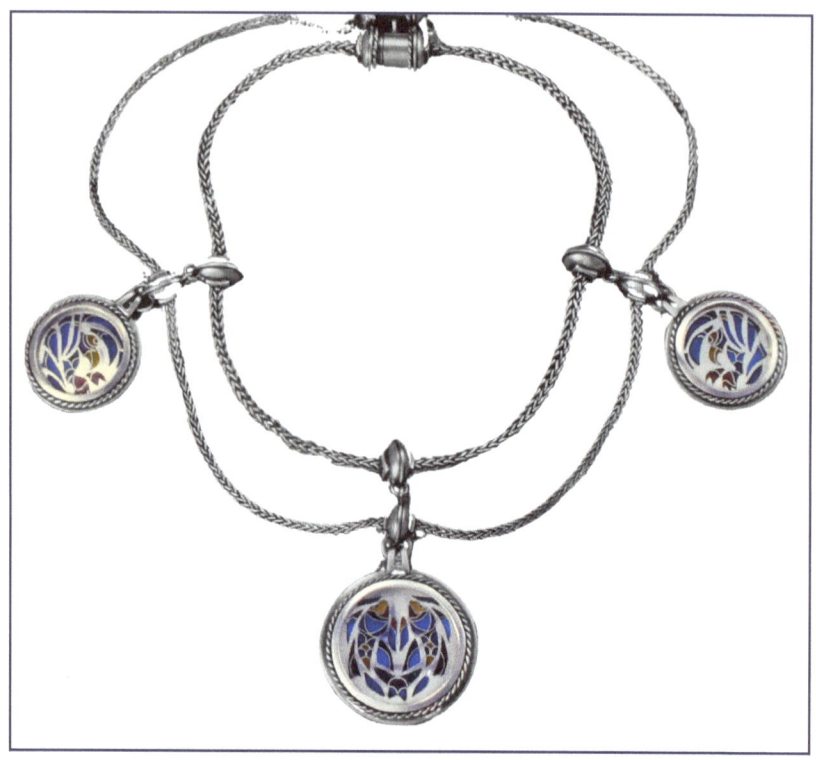

Champleve and Cloisonne Enamel "Byzantine" Necklace, 1976, hand woven chain

Woven chain Scarab Bracelet, 1976

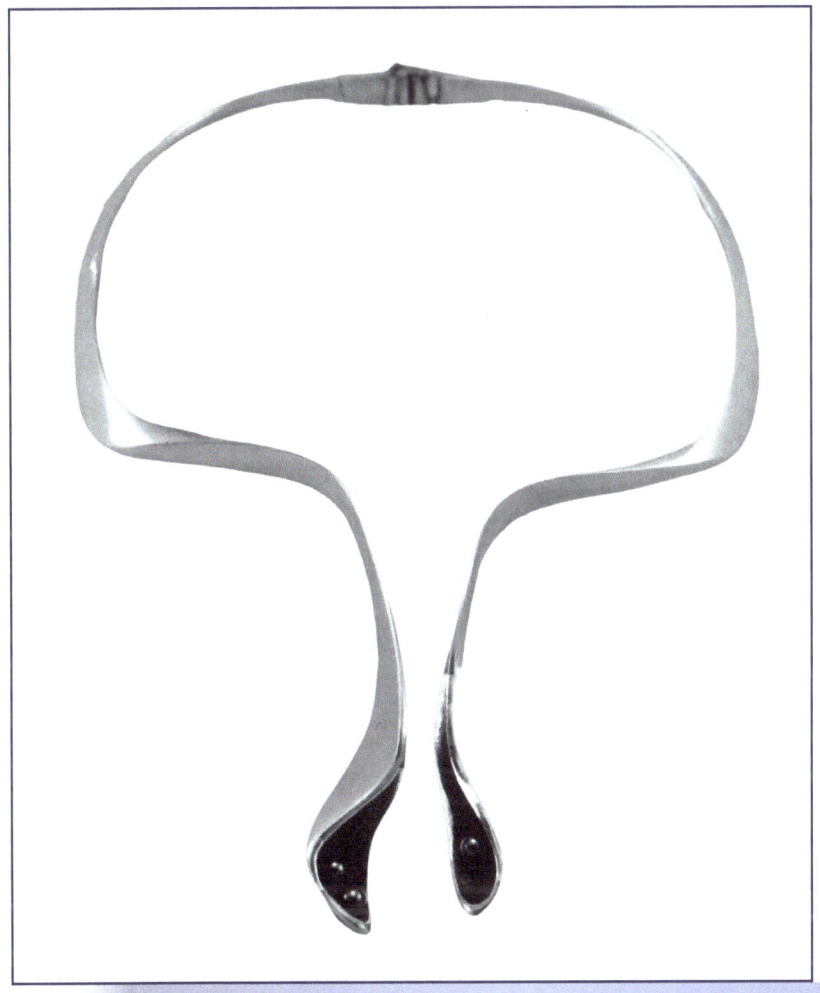

Forged Silver choker w/black pearls, 1970

Hollow Form Silver and Delrin Bracelet, 1978

It wasn't long before I realized I was no candidate for the corporate world of jewelry production. I just didn't fit in, and I couldn't compete, nor did I want to. Soon I tapped into the secretarial skills my mother forced me to take in high school, insisting that I never be forced to depend upon a man. I found a job working at "The Typettes" where I could make my own hours transcribing letters and cassette tapes. The business was in my favorite building, The Flatiron Building on 23rd St. Mindy, the owner, was a lovely woman who looked and spoke like the actress Melanie Griffith. Mindy fancied herself an inventor and spent her days designing packaging disguised as gift wrapping. She would invent and I would type. She paid me well, even when there were no jobs at hand. Sometimes she would send me out to shop or explore the area on her own dime and time. I found that by working part-time jobs unrelated to my passion helped me selfishly save my creativity and let it grow.

Meanwhile, I was desperate for a place to create. I would walk SoHo and midtown looking for jewelry schools, eager to rent bench time so I could work with my hands and create some pieces I had brewing inside me. Eventually, I found a small school in midtown, Studio Jewelers, that would allow me to exchange bench time if I'd clean the studio. This worked out well for over two years and I started to make stage wear for my friends who were starting bands. That was fun and I met a large array of different people at this school. There was Alan, the forensic detective who would regale me with stories of the most recent NYC crimes and Abe, the young Hasidic man who had intense body odor and didn't have the least amount of soldering aptitude. The biggest gift of all, however, was that I was able to create in my spare time.

Eventually, my boyfriend, Stephen, began working as an art designer for Carlos Falchi, a handbag designer and manufacturer. He would come home with scraps of leather and exotic skins, and I began to make belts and cuffs in leather and metal. I made a rubber and leather outfit (shoes, belt, hat and dress) for my friend Cynthia and she walked the runway at the Javits Center for World Art Day. Since I come from Akron, Ohio, (Rubber City, rubber capitol of the world) working with rubber seemed like a pun on my origin because I grew up with the smell of burning rubber in my nostrils.

Carlos Falchi, thinking about his leather creations

JOB HUNTING

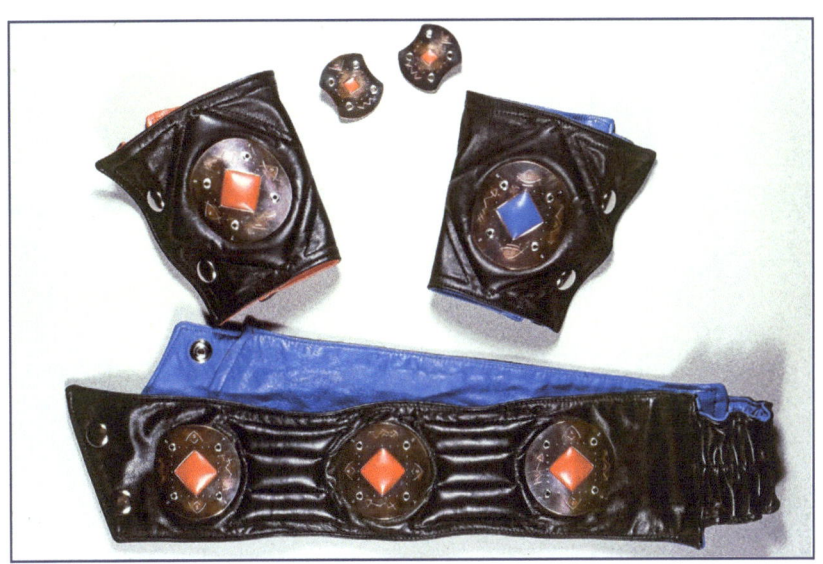

Leather Cuff, Belt and Earrings with copper, 1982

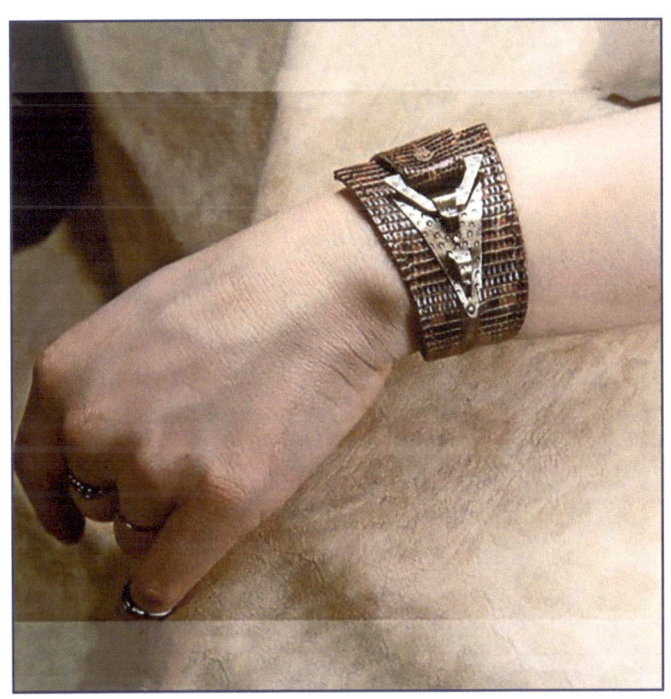

Lizard and bronze wristband, 1982, fabricated

Cynthia Sley, singer for band Bush Tetras in my rubber outfit, 1984

At Studio Jewelers I met some fellow metalsmiths and jewelers. We decided to rent a workspace together on 38th St. I bought a leather sewing machine and began purchasing full skins of leather from Carlos. He taught me "trapunto", the stuffing of the leather with poly fiberfill and sewing around them to created little puffs of sensuality. I'd add copper and silver and often engrave the metal with graffiti I'd seen in the subways. Sometimes I'd add stones to the metal and rivet them to the leather pieces. My prize invention was the Pouch Belt which was widely slung on the hip and contained hidden pockets. The pouch belts had elastic on the side with loops that resembled bullet loops. I used them to hold my tubes of lipstick. It was the '80's when tunics, spandex pants and huge belts mixed with a lot of heavy metal were ruling fashion and streetwear.

In 1980, at the 38th Street shared studio located on the top floor, I had created a collection of Pouch Belts which were lying on the top of my workbench. A night burglar broke in through the window and stole all my belts and stuffed them with the gemstones from the benches of my studio mates. We were devastated at the loss, but this experience taught each of us a lesson on the necessity of security gates in NYC.

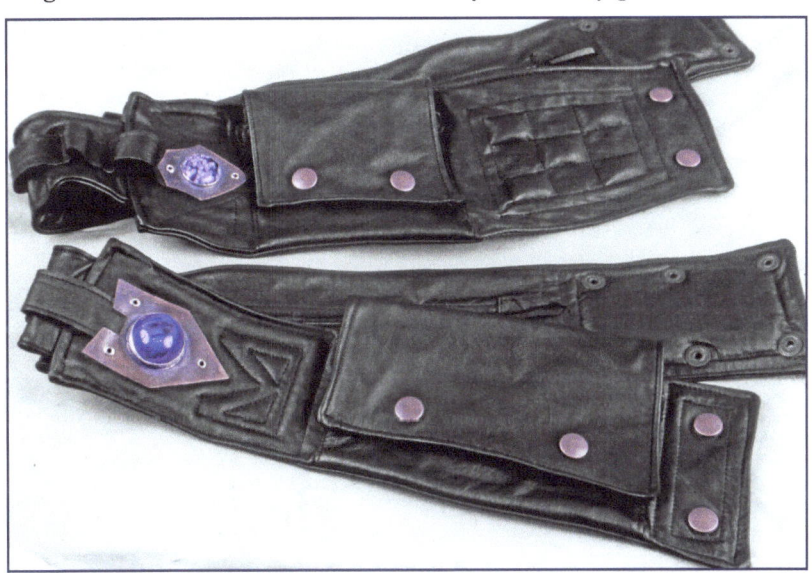

Pouch Belts, Buffalo Skin with Copper and Semi-Precious Stones, bought by Barney's 1990

Annie Lennox in Leather Suit. My belt, 1984

JOB HUNTING

In the early 80's my leather and metal work had gained a following. Annie Lennox was a friend of Cynthia Sley's, with whom I'd moved from Cleveland to NYC. Cynthia was and still is lead singer for the Bush Tetras, a legendary 80's punk band. Annie came into my 7th Street store and asked me to put metal on her leather jumpsuit and add a belt for the outfit. Imagine my surprise when she went into my bathroom, stripped down to her white, French lace underwear, and came out to put on her leather jumpsuit. I couldn't believe my eyes. She was so incredibly beautiful and talented; I was in awe. That leather outfit took center stage during her "Missionary Man" tour.

In 1984, I started my wholesale business using the name "Clear Metals". My last name, Klar, means clear in German and I love the concept of clarity. Thinking one day I would live to see transparent metals; I enjoyed this pun. I began selling to stores and one of my largest orders was placed by Barney's. It was my first $15,000 order and they ordered my Pouch Belts and Jewelry. After the order was delivered, Barney filed for bankruptcy and 8 months later, I still had not been paid. My sales partner began calling them for payment every day. In her last phone call to them, I heard her say, "The next time you hear from me, I'll be sitting in your offices in NJ, handcuffed to a chair until we get paid. I have a few books I haven't had time to read." We were paid the next week.

If I had free time, I loved to shop for materials. Although I had little money to buy supplies, I could be found digging through metal scraps at Canal Metals or plastic shapes at Canal Plastic. At that time there were fun places to shop in NYC that had industrial surplus. Once I bought plastic tubing at Canal Rubber and filled it with small plastic trinkets floating in colored water. I was shocked when Pat Field bought them for her store on 8th St. I knew her to be a true visionary.

Little by little, I'd discover shops or galleries to which I imagined might buy my work. Barney's, Bergdorf's and Bendel's would have "open days" where a designer could stand in line and meet with accessory buyers. I did this as often as possible and during one of these events at Bergdorf's, the buyer ordered my hammered large Wing Earrings which were later purchased for Lena Horne by her stylist when she had her show on Broadway. Broke and depressed, imagine my surprise when I was watching Good Morning America on TV and saw Lena wearing them during an interview as promo for her Broadway show, "LENA!". Immediately I wrote a fan letter to her and included another pair of these earrings and sent them to the theatre. She was incredibly kind and thanked me with a letter in response. This was the first of many signed celebrity photos that would become displayed on what I would call my "NYC Deli Wall" in my future SoHo store. Later, these same earrings were purchased by Wim Wenders for his lead actress in "Wings of Desire" when Jim Jarmusch brought him by my East Village store.

During this time when I was attempting to scrape a living together by making jewelry, I retained my passion for art jewelry. Jewelry that was fun and wearable, but unique and unusual. I was delighted when 3 of my art jewelry pins were accepted into a show on 57th St. held in the famous "Aaron Faber" Gallery. Immediately one of these pins was sold by the gallery and its wholesale cost was $60. It took them 6 months to pay me for this piece and I had to call them a minimum of 6 times requesting payment. This was shocking to me, and it was, sadly, the first of many retail & gallery experiences.

The 3 pins submitted to a show at Aaron Faber Gallery on 57th st.

[6] Tiffany's

Growing up in the wasteland of Ohio, I never knew about Tiffany's until I saw the movie "Breakfast at Tiffany's" when I was a teenager. Like every young girl, I wanted to be Holly Go Lightly. Her elegance and her tempered sarcasm were a balm to my aspirations when I entered puberty. Even though I knew I could never be as feminine as Audrey Hepburn or *Holly*, I studied her grace and style. More than that, the "little blue box" held a fairy tale romance I never knew existed.

Many years later, when I moved to NYC and went to the Met and saw Lois Comfort Tiffany's lamps, silver, and glass I was inspired to learn more about him. His work was crafted with perfection and his expertise in designing a range of crafts was limitless. I developed a deep fascination with his history and much to my surprise, I found myself moving into a loft in the old Tiffany studios with my boyfriend Stephen. This building, across from the Metropolitan Life Building at 333 Park Avenue South had been home to Tiffany's Glass Studios at the turn of the century. I felt as if I was permitted entrance into a magical part of history when I moved into this loft. This 4-story red brick building took up most of the block on the east side of Park Ave. between 26th and 27th street. It was now lofts and it seemed that every time construction or renovation occurred within these walls, a new Tiffany Factory Artifact was discovered: Frosted and etched letter windows that had been on the doors of the printing department. Mahogany and ebony inlayed shelving on the top floor of the building, which had been L.C.T.'s original office. My boyfriend had been given the gift of renting two lofts in this historic building because they were owned by my boyfriend's employer, Carlos Falchi, the handbag designer. Carlos owned these lofts, but no longer lived in the building. We had one loft as a living space and the other had two working spaces. The space I had was over 20 ft. tall with an 8-foot angled and peaked skylight. This space was everything I wanted it to be, my atelier in NYC! My friend Charlie built a long catwalk around the perimeter of the space for my leather working and below I had my workbench and large table with a steel restaurant sink my boyfriend's brother had found and installed for me. At night, when I was working, I felt a palpable excitement in the air with clapping hands of joy that made me feel as if I was continuing in the tradition of making. At first, I was spooked when I would catch a tall figure out of the corner of my eye or feel a tap on my shoulder in the shadows from the skylight and no one was there. Eventually, I came to embrace these sightings as joyful encouragement.

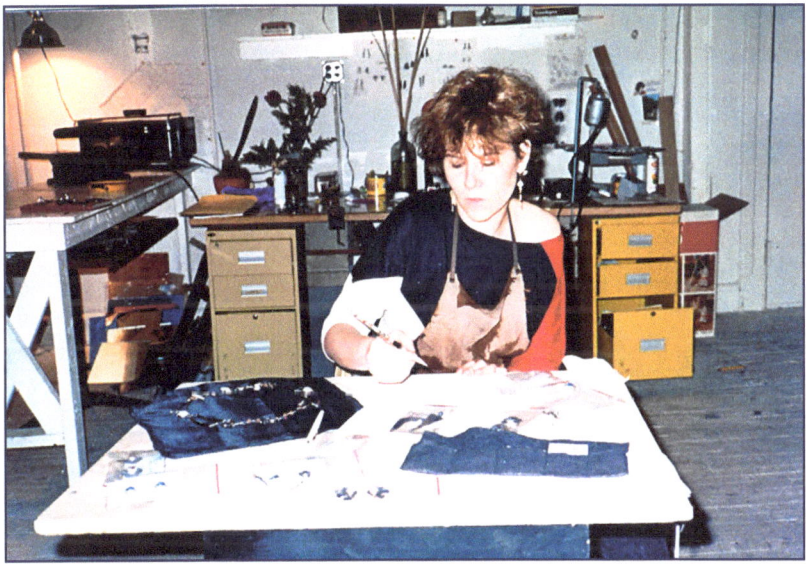

BK in Tiffany Glass Studio, 1982

"YOU'RE SO TALENTED"

TIFFANY'S

BK Studio, 1982, in the Tiffany Glass Studios, 333 Park Ave. South

"YOU'RE SO TALENTED"

"Lense" Necklace. Fabricated Sterling, Bronze, recycled Ivory, copper (pictured on table, above)

Fueling the joy of working in this former Tiffany Studio was the experience I had in 1981 when I visited my former art school mate, Jane, while she was working in Newark at the end of the era for the Tiffany Factory in Newark, NJ. This factory housed the expanding sterling silver & stationery manufacturing departments of the world-famous jewelry store until 1985. I was told that originally it had been a hydro-powered factory that was shipped to America from England by L.C. Tiffany and rebuilt in Newark in 1892.

Taking the bus to Newark from Manhattan, I watched through the windows as I viewed the deteriorating manufacturing landscapes void of people and full of debris. Getting off at the bus top I meandered up a path until I reached a meadow surrounded by pastel houses like nesting shoeboxes. All the employee houses were around a football field sized meadow that featured a red brick castle which was the Tiffany Factory.

I was to meet my friend in the hollowware department but before the era of cellphones, we had not arranged a meeting time or place. When I walked through the Tudor door to the factory, I was astounded that there were no employees on the ground floor. I ran my fingers across the giant flatware stamping machines that were silent and ghostly in their magnificence. I found the stairs at the end of the giant room with high ceilings to accommodate these machines and walked past the robin's egg blue door that said "Boxes and Stationery" on the front. I gently opened the door and saw walls of blue boxes and spools of white ribbons. Scissors were left on the large central table as if abandoned during assembly.

When I found Jane on the third floor, she greeted me in a room the size of a gymnasium which was rimmed with 10-foot windows and featured a 12-foot diameter annealing station. The annealing station had smaller rotating annealing pans on the perimeter with huge torches at every station capable of annealing and softening the large hollowware the master craftsmen repaired and maintained. Jane's co-workers were all men in their late 50's and early 60's who wore muslin work aprons and shook my hand kindly as I entered their realm. I thought and wished I could be taken in as a team member, but this factory was sadly in its final stages of decline. They showed me the walk-in safe where every original model for a piece of jewelry or hollowware was stored. Dumbfounded and struck by awe, I left disappointed and heartbroken in this stunning example of historical deterioration and loss. Heading back to the bus stop, I cursed myself that I had been born too late to take part in this rich tradition. Today I am sad, yet relieved to know the building remains and has been converted to a condominium complex, Tiffany Manor, by a private developer.

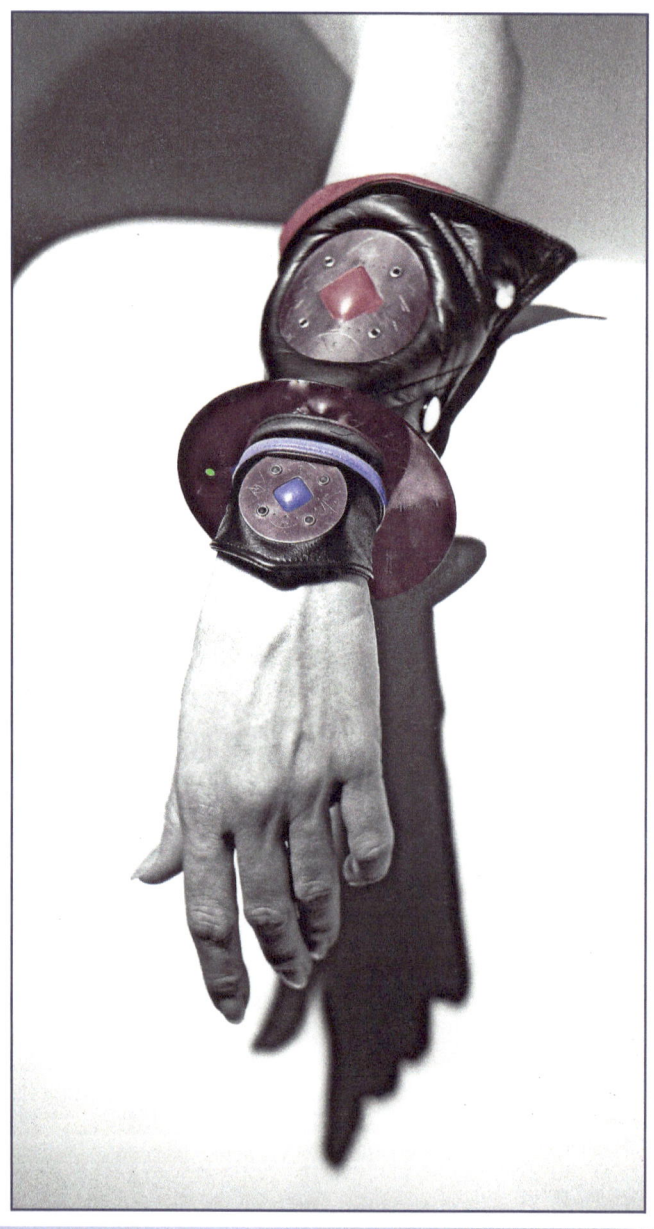

Leather Bracelets and "African Knife" Bracelet, copper, 1982
Photo by Stephen Black

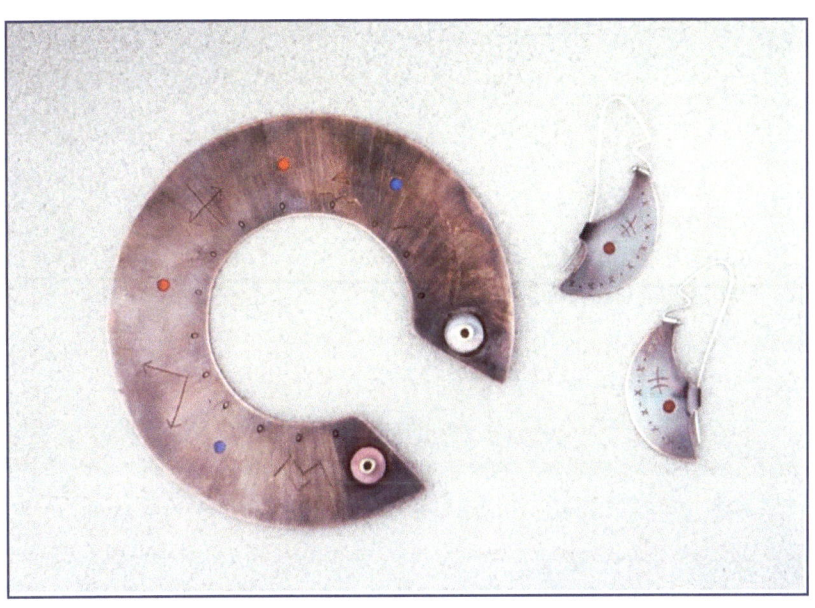

Copper "African Knife" Bracelet, Earrings, plexiglass inlay, 1982

[7] Artwear, 1981

I first spotted Artwear while I was schlepping a suitcase full of jewelry that I had made around SoHo. I was looking for other jewelry artists and their studios, hoping to find somewhere that I could pull up a chair to a bench and work. I had no money, yet I was imagining that I could clean someone's studio in exchange for bench time.

The large windows caught my attention from across the street and I was pulled to the store like a magnet. I stood outside, afraid to enter such a wonderful, beautiful, intimidating world. I'd never seen such interesting metalwork displayed as art. Art to Wear. Artwear. "What IS this place?" I wondered. Soon I began to hear about Robert Lee Morris. He was the first jewelry designer who taught the world to think of jewelry as art outside of the box. Robert created this concept of Art to Wear. I felt as though I had found a kindred spirit who I didn't even know. He created a magical and wondrous world of which I wanted to be a part.

It wasn't long before I heard through the grapevine that Robert held "open Sundays" at ArtWear and this is how they worked: An aspiring jewelry designer would stand in line with samples in hand and have a look-see with Robert. It was formal. The line was long, and no one talked. I was nervous and overwhelmed. Soon it was my turn and Robert was very silent, handsome, and tall. He looked at my work intently, turning it in his hands and peering at every detail, every flaw. At the time, I had been working freelance for Carlos Falchi, collecting scraps of his leather bags in pinks, blues, reds, and black. I would sew the skins together, stuff them with trapunto, and rivet shapes of copper and silver with semi-precious gemstones onto these creations to make large gauntlets, cuffs, and belts. I would engrave the metal with "graffiti" symbols I had picked up from the streets of the East Village. These pieces were a true testament to the 80's in NYC.

Robert suggested quietly but firmly that I should do this and change that. He looked at me and never smiled. He said I could come back once I had made these changes and meet with him again. I left, crushed. I went back to my studio and stomped around for a bit. I didn't get it; this was MY vision! Through my stomping, I realized that it was all a

BK, 1980 in the subway on my way to first gallery show where some of her work was shown, photo by Stephen Black

game and if I wanted to play it, I had to be in it. After a week of this, I realized he had insight, and I made his suggested changes. Another open Sunday session and he greeted my effort with a clap of his hands and invited me into his gallery for a collective show. I was overjoyed! This was the very first time I began to sell my work and develop a collection. This was the beginning.

Two years later, the end of this gallery relationship with Robert taught me another lesson: That nothing is original. I had begun creating bracelets and earrings that were shaped like disks, based on African Knife Bracelets, which had their edges sharpened and were used for fighting. Minus the sharpened edges, mine were made of disks of copper, engraved with graffiti, and inlaid with acrylic. 18 months into my tenure with Artwear, I was no longer selling and my checks from them for sales had ceased. When I walked into the gallery and saw my friend Sally, a sales associate, I said, "Sally, why is my work not selling?" She looked down at her feet as she whispered, "Robert moved your work into the cabinets, out of view." "Why?" I asked her. Silently she walked me around to Robert's large case of his own work and there were his versions of my African Knife Bracelets, which had never been my designs in the first place. Indignant and too young to digest the insignificance of my own originality, I withdrew my work and my design presence at Artwear.

I will always credit Robert Lee Morris for raising our collective jewelry consciousness. Jewelry became Art to Wear. This is the art that is worn closest to the body. And thank you, Robert, for giving me my first break. It's been the ride of a lifetime and although I've loved every minute of it, lessons can be difficult. It's a learning curve.

[8] 7th Street

We had been together four years, but we were only married for four months. I should have known that I considered it more of a business relationship than a romantic one when I found myself wearing a tie and a white shirt under a bulky sweater at the civil ceremony. I considered this a marriage of equals that would prove opportune for each of us. In my mind, I thought we both needed and wanted this. With little input from him, I'd had two abortions and thought we were on the same page striving towards the coupledom of artistic expression and freedom. Stephen was from a broken family, and I never knew he wanted his own. We didn't communicate because at 30 we were still emotionally unequipped. When he chose his next long-term partner as a younger woman with whom he worked, I felt horrified and betrayed. It took me years to realize that the betrayal had been mine all along because I'd killed his babies.

From the Tiffany loft to a mental explosion of alternatives, I didn't know how to proceed. I thought about switching coasts and moving to Hollywood where I imagined I could work in the design department for Star Trek or another science fiction series. Or perhaps I could move to Paris and camp on the steps of Thierry Mugler or John Paul Gaultier, begging them to hire me. But in reality, I chose to stay closer to home and continue to ride the roller coaster life of NYC with my circle of friends.

Searching the rental classifieds in The Village Voice, I found a live-work situation in the East Village on 7th Street between 1st Avenue and Avenue A.

It was next to the Ukrainian Church and a door away from their Funeral Parlor.

Several small artsy designers had also moved onto this treelined block and I was delighted that the previous tenant had renovated the store with a sleeping loft, exposed brick walls and a bathtub. At the time, "fixture fees" were common and the previous tenant was asking a $10K fee for all his renovations. Perhaps out of guilt for leaving me or perhaps because his mother liked me so much, Stephen's mother agreed to loan me the money. It took me almost 5 years to repay the loan.

I arranged the store like a tightly organized ship. The storefront was about 250 square feet, and I shared a bathroom with the small independent gallery next door. I brought the steel restaurant sink from the loft and made the front part of the store my showroom, the middle part my workshop and the sleeping loft my bedroom. My business office education came in handy when I discovered that I could work during the week at a temp agency, work at night in my studio and open the store to the public on weekends. This became my life.

I struggled to pay the rent. Sales were non-existent to slim, and I only realized that people desired my work when I noticed it was getting stolen. Unable to afford theft insurance, I developed a sly system to capture thieves. I had a double-cylinder lock installed on my front door. When I suspected someone shoplifting, I would walk over to the door, lock it inconspicuously and remove the key so we were locked in. I would then grab the iron "pull down" bar which I used for the outside gate and approach them quietly and say, "I think you have something of mine." Necessity is the mother of invention.

I had a white cat, Olivia, who was beautiful with shining emerald eyes, and I'd get annoyed when people would only stop by to visit her. People would visit the same pieces of jewelry over and over until one finally came in with a wad of cash in her pocket and said, "I've decided not to pay my rent this month because I've been dreaming of that ring for so many months!" I didn't know if I should smile or frown and tried to talk her out of it. "Are you sure? That seems a little scary," I said. She blankly replied, "Something always comes up" as she calmly handed me the cash.

My cat Olivia, wearing a necklace I'd made for her

Olivia's Necklace, 1977, Silver & Copper, inlay, woven chain, shells

BK in front of first store on 7th St., NYC

I lived a life full of wild nights and exciting days at that store. It was full of impromptu parties, spilling onto the street and hanging out at King Tut's Wa Wa Hut or the Pyramid Club around the corner. Some nights as I was undressing and slipping into bed, I felt extremely vulnerable living "on the street" as friends and acquaintances would shake and bang on the gates shouting, "Barbara, are you in there?" I would hide and pretend I wasn't there because that was the only way I could get any peace.

Lydia Lunch with Cross Pendant in a fashion show at Limelight, 1984

Quietly, yet quickly it seemed my store gained a following. Annie Lennox dropped by my store. Luc (now Lucy) Sante would stop by and talk, smoking their Galoise Cigarettes blithely. Klaus Nomi would stop by and slouch on my chair as he adjusted his pointy black hair and wild attire. Cindy Lauper came in asking for Infinity Sign charms. One day Jim Jarmusch brought his pal Wim Wenders into the store.

Lena Horne in her Broadway Show, "Lena: The Lady and Her Music", 1981

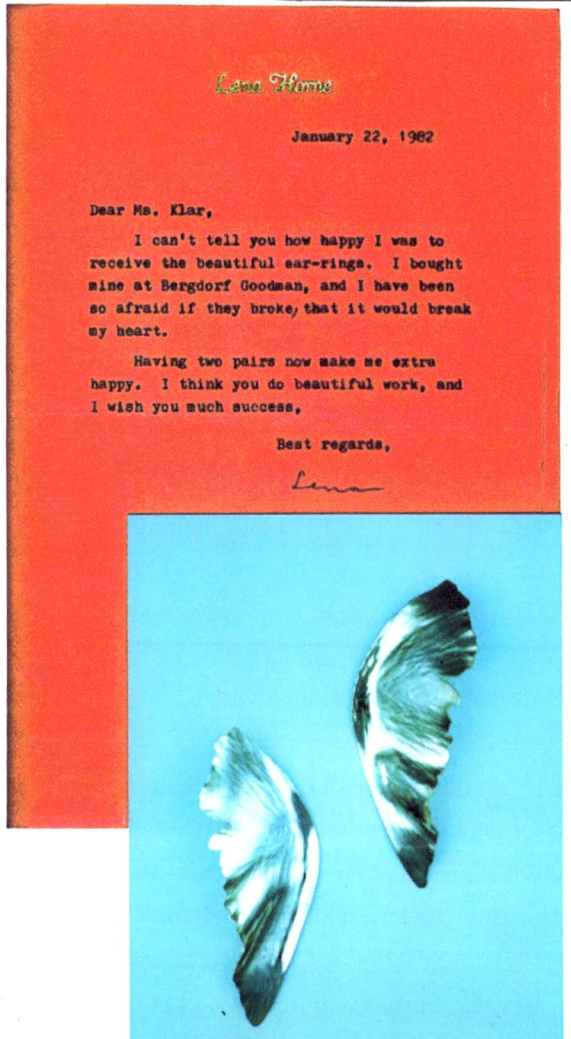

Looking back, these hammered wing earrings were my first sign that things could get interesting for me.

I've always considered myself to be a fan of pop-culture and creativity. I liked to give away as much of my work as I could and not to just anybody. I called it "creating a following". I wanted to see people wearing it and I also subscribed to the notion that there is a full circle of giving and receiving. Once I stood in line for hours at Tower Records when Tina Turner was signing her latest album, Private Dancer. I had made her a black patent leather belt dripping in red rhinestones and she couldn't have been more gracious. I don't know if she ever wore it but that pales in comparison to the joy her music has brought me.

I think Press is important. It's obvious that nothing sells in America like fame. Free press is the best. Someone once told me that to be a designer, one had to make people want to BE them. They should want to have your life. I would roll my eyes and shrug my shoulders but ultimately that is the case. When a client or a friend tells me how successful they think I am, I always say, "Yeah, but it's all done with mirrors".

Then the ceiling fell in. Literally. My lease was over and there was a new owner who was intent on gentrifying the neighborhood further. I met with him and was honest that I was thinking of moving but I wasn't quite ready to do it just yet. Standing in his polished shoes he said to me, "please sign the new lease, I promise I'll let you out of it when you're ready. You see, my partner's son really wants the space but it's a conflict of interest for me and a situation I'd rather avoid."

New to this game of NYC business deals, I was unaware that I had just shaken hands with the devil.

Months passed and apartment after apartment in the building were vacated. I saw older tenants being pushed out through lack of electricity and heat. Eventually the apartment above my store became vacant and the renovations began. Before I knew it, a debris chute had been placed above my front door and debris was being thrown down on a regular basis. People couldn't get into my front door. One day, I came back from errands and my workbench full of tiny silver pieces waiting to be assembled was covered in fallen material from my ceiling. My rack of fine leathers was soaked in water due to a leak coming from above. I was beside myself and spent hours calling the management office to no avail. One day, a client came into the store and asked me what was going on. I explained the situation to her, and she said to me, "You know, what is happening here is something called constructive eviction. I'm a real estate lawyer and your landlord is making your business impossible." On the spot I hired her with a small retaining fee, and she advised me to move out, break the lease, and give the keys to my landlord. I followed her advice, and I moved out within the week.

But the landlord resisted and sued me. Apparently, he had forgotten our deal, and he wouldn't return my phone calls and I had no physical address for his business. The lawsuit lasted 3 years and cost me $15,000 in 1989. Even though I'd had a good case with evidence in my favor, it would have cost me another $30K to pursue my lawsuit. To preserve my mental health, I realized it had to stop even though it was unjust. I struggled to pay off that $15k for 7 years.

[9] The Story of the Aegis

In 1984 East 7th street was a beautiful out-of-the way Ukrainian neighborhood that transformed itself into a hotbed of activity in the late hours. My store, Clear Metals, was tightly nestled between a funeral home and a church. There was so much local color here that gentrification was not initially welcomed. It wasn't long before I realized I was, unknowingly, a part of that gentrification.

When I moved into my store, the sounds of the night were disruptive and scary. I would hear mumblings and rumblings of the passersby who seemed as if they were standing inside my space. It was disconcerting and a little terrifying when I began to find playing cards strewn in my entryway every morning. Upon closer inspection, I noticed they had been scribbled upon in black marker with sayings like "Out Eurotrash" and "Go Back". As a young woman living alone "on the street", I was deeply troubled.

One day my friend Illythe came to visit, and I showed her the cards. She looked at them and seemed to understand. She said, "Wait, I'm going to Israel tomorrow and I will bring you back something that will make whoever is doing this, STOP."

Several weeks went by and the cards continued to appear. Illythe visited again, fresh from her Israel trip and gave me a small package, which was wrapped in brown paper and twine. She said, "This will protect you. Hang it where they can see it".

This was my first experience with the Hand of Protection. The one she gave me was about 6 inches tall in Blue Glass, a blob of glass with the imprint of a hand. The hand had an eye in its palm and the entire piece was heavy and about 7 inches in length with a hole in the top for hanging. I hung it near the doorway and the playing cards never appeared in my entryway again. I've carried that Hand of Protection with me since 1984 and displayed it in every studio, home and store I have inhabited. I feel it has enveloped me in what I call the "white light of protection."

Glass "Hand of Fatima" from Israel, 1984

In the tradition of a Mezuzah, the Hand of Fatima, and any other Talisman you can think of, I have called my creation the Aegis (pronounced eye--guss). It took me over a year to perfect this version of the hand and it is covered in a symbology I have developed as my own personal hieroglyphs. I have carved these "glyphs" into jewelry and art over the years and developed their meanings into something that is personal and initially derived from other cultures. A list of the symbols and their meanings follows.

I have always felt that I needed all the protection I could get. It's scary out there. I wish you the white light of protection in your life, always.

My version, called the Aegis, 2006 (pronounced eye-gus)

Here is one of my hang tags explaining all the symbols I use:

Clear Metals
www.clearmetals.com
introduces Aegis
'The Hand of Protection'

not actual size

Aegis is shown here in Pewter with a Pink Gold Plated Heart
Style no. PA100pg

Aegis is also available in Pewter with a Yellow Gold Plated Heart
Style no. PA100yg

Both are priced at $23.00
and measure 2 1/4 w x 4 1/8 h

This Pewter hand is a Talisman to protect the home and those who reside in it. Aegis 'The Hand of Protection'

Inquiries~Orders~Sales tel>fax: 845 626 3700
barbara@clearmetals.com

© Clear Metals 2010

- 🜛 Eternal, All-Seeing Eye, Protection
- ☆ Bird: Movement, Change, Travel
- 〜 Water: Movement, Change
- ∞ Infinity, Inspiration, Creation
- ～ Feather~Leaf: Lightness of Being, Truth
- ☆ Star: Fame, White Light, Guidance
- ☾ Moon: Renewel, Taper
- ✕ Multiplication, Increase
-  Crossed Arrows: Peace, Guidance, Protection
- ♡ Heart, Harmony
- ҉ Spiral, Creation, Centered Strentgh

© Clear Metals 2010

[10] Symbols

My first reaction to NYC in 1979 was the wall paintings and proliferous graffiti. It was bold and messaged a secret world of color and injustice. SAMO graffiti (Jean-Michel Basquiat) was everywhere as well as the graffiti of Keith Haring and Kenny Sharf. In narrow passageways and alcoves everywhere I looked there were graffiti tags and symbols that were curious. When I opened my store in 1984, I began hand-engraving symbols into metal and carving symbols into waxwork. I developed my own language for symbols and eventually created a small hang tag that had examples of all the symbols I used in my work.

In 1989 I attended a UFO abduction meeting hosted by the artist and UFO enthusiast Bud Hopkins. Bud went over the sightings around NYC and several attendees told their stories. It was a small group of about 30 people and at the end he handed all of us a piece of paper and pen: we were to draw any symbols we could pull from our memory. After the close of the meeting, he asked about 4 of us to hold back and he told us that it was very possible we had been abducted. I was not surprised because I'd had several dreams where I was aboard spaceships which seemed astoundingly real. It is reported that there are symbols on the sides and interiors of captured UFO's that are mysterious. If you've never seen the movie, "Hanger 18", https://en.wikipedia.org/wiki/Hangar_18_(film), you might want to check it out as it is supposedly based on a captured UFO that was hidden and reverse-engineered at Wright-Patterson Airforce Base in Dayton, Ohio.

To me, symbols represent a silent light of protection and intention. They are as ancient as the beginning of the world, and we all have our own favorite symbols. I think it is naturally human.

Graffiti Rings, 1984, Sterling, gold, ruby, sapphire

Cynthia Sley's Drawing of BK, 2017

SYMBOLS

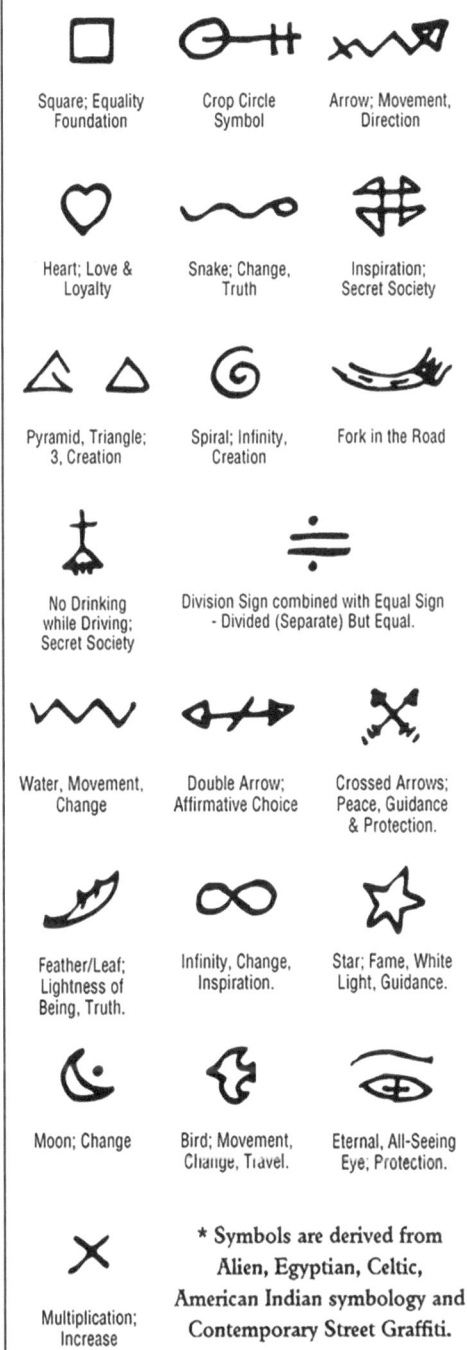

[11] Moving the Store to SoHo

By 1988 the East Village was rapidly changing. Rents were going up and gentrification was increasing. During that time, I slowly realized I wanted to open a store in SoHo. SoHo had art and fashion that seemed to line the streets. I hired a business consultant to help me write a business proposal. I went on to present this proposal to all my clients who I thought might believe in me and be interested in investing. I offered them payback plus interest after two years OR payback plus a share of the profits after two years. They all chose the latter, and I was able to raise $20K to open my new store on Thompson St. in SoHo. At the time, the building was in bank receivership, and I got so nervous when they kept stalling the presentation of the lease that I offered to go in and type it up myself when the management company said the delay was due to their lack of a secretary. I became that secretary again.

When I signed the lease, I wore my big cubic zirconia ring that looked like a huge diamond. I signed my name with the rose gold pen my girlfriend Rebeca had given me for good luck.

My friends were my biggest supporters. Painters painted my walls with faux finishes, and I had the ceiling framed with a painting of clouds and birds in flight. A local contractor friend made cases around the perimeter of the store, and I made all the handles for these cases out of bronze and copper. I accented the space with some vintage jewelry cases and oriental rugs. Of course, there had to be a vintage Art Deco couch for those people worn out by shopping that were accompanying their wives, husbands, friends, and lovers. I even got a small child's vintage desk for a line of pet tags I made, hoping the pets could see them at eye level.

At the time, Thompson Street was off the beaten path in Soho. I was surprised when students, potential jewelry designers, and jewelers looking to open stores kept stopping by and asking me business questions. I was confused because I didn't consider myself an expert of any kind. I had always just blindly moved forward.

I was surprised when 3 other jewelry stores opened on Thompson Street within the first 2 years I was there. At first, I was horrified because I thought it would dilute the popularity of my store, but I learned that in reality it added to the interest of the street and became "destination jewelry shopping". Many times, shoppers would come to my store first and then say they were going to shop the street after looking at my work. Nine times out of ten, they'd come back for a purchase. I like to think that there is a market for everything and that by holding fast to my instincts I could stand out in the crowd.

I felt powerful in those moments when the money was exchanging hands and people would say, "Wow, I can see you're doing really well, Barbara, you've certainly made it!"

I would feel important when I was accepted at the head of the line in a crowded and famous local eatery like Nick and Toni's even though no one suspected that everything was a constant struggle. It seemed every time I was able to stand, I was knocked to my knees again and again. I also learned that nothing could teach me about money like not having any.

By 1998 I had 7 employees, a retail store in SoHo, and a workshop/home in Williamsburg, Brooklyn. I was working constantly and could barely keep up with the demands of employees, clients, and commissions.

While I was creating avant-garde adornment for a fashion show, people were unaware that payroll was overdue. Or that Mickey Rourke had just stolen 3 of my one-of-a-kind rings from a fashion shoot. The temporary thrills I had when I saw my work on the cover of a magazine or worn by Sean Young in "Wall Street" were minimized by the need to work 24 hours a day, 7 days a week.

The guilt I felt when I chose to stay home and rest was often interrupted by a panicked phone call with a request for a social appearance or with an unimaginable jewelry emergency when their favorite ring was run over by a truck on Park Avenue.

When people would walk by my store in SoHo and peer into the windows during the frosty Christmas shopping season in 1999, they would see glittering jewels in a beautiful space full of beautiful people. Someone on the outside looking in wouldn't know that the bank had just pulled my $15K CD to repay my overdraft without my permission. They didn't know that Barney's refused to pay me for a $15K wholesale order when they filed for bankruptcy.

Outsiders weren't aware that my designs were being stolen. They didn't see the dissolved partnerships or the glittery fashion friends who eventually ghosted me.

Clear Metals Store, Thompson St., SoHo, NYC 1993 Valentine's Day

Clear Metals, Store Interior

There was a way not to worry about money ever again. I could do what my contemporaries were doing; selling their designs on QVC and buying ranches in New Mexico. These artists were building empires and when the opportunity came to have my designs made overseas through QVC, I realized the last thing I wanted to become was a manufacturer overseeing a bigger business. If I did that, I knew my creativity would take a backseat to managing a business.

Plus, it seemed to me like a deal with the devil: Trading my creativity for cash. When I stood in front of the QVC studio heads and I saw them nodding and whispering to each other, I overheard them saying, "Do you think her work is commercial enough? Do you think her presence would be acceptable on air or is she too quirky?" I couldn't bring myself to go that route and lose my time behind the bench as a metalsmith which was so treasured like my time with my father in his basement workshop.

Gradually, a little bird appeared on my shoulder telling me that something was coming. When the stock market fell and all my Wall Street clients holding wads of cash disappeared, I became agitated and panicked. I was working so hard, but I instinctively felt an anticipation of dread. I imagined a bus or a taxi would hit me as I blindly walked into oncoming traffic while my mind was racing with my tasks at hand.

[12] The Clients

They were slyly stalking the store. At first, it was just weekends, then it became almost daily. He wore a tailored business suit, but I could see the tattoos peeking out from under his white shirt. He saw me as I took his inventory and peered at me through his John Lennon spectacles. She walked a step behind him and wore a pink ruffled dress that was retro and quirky. Her hair was curly, her body curvaceous, and she had full lips that screamed red lipstick.

He extended his hand and gently said, "Hi I'm Ira and this is Lizzy". "Nice to meet you," I said. They both looked down into the bracelet case and Ira stated he loved my work and had a special project for me. "Can you make me a bracelet like the one Keith Richards always wears?" I suddenly felt a tingle in my stomach, the one I always get when I try to conceal my enthusiasm. I'd been studying that bracelet for years and had even sourced the jeweler in London who'd made it. Keith never took it off, it was in every photo shoot and every video. Ira asked to see a heavy link bracelet from the case.

Ira knew his jewelry. I can always tell when someone is a jewelry whore. They look closely, turn the pieces over, look at the back, and study the architecture and mechanics of every solder seam, hinge, and clasp. He lifted his glasses for closer inspection. Lizzy peered over Ira's shoulder and exhaled long, admiring sighs in a girly breathlessness. "I love that other one there. It looks so Gothic". I never liked it when someone opened the cases on their own and helped themselves. Too many hands in too many directions made me nervous. "Here, let me help you", I said, but it was too late. She had several bracelets out of the case simultaneously and was putting them on Ira all in one swift motion. It was plain for me to see that Lizzy was not only quiet and overtly feminine but one who should be studied for their subtle strength and agendas. Ira tugged at his shirt and jacket revealing a tattooed sleeve that was swirling with color and content. "I like these two, I'll take them". I was trying to stop time and allow those words to make my heart dance, but before I realized, his other hand dove into his pants and pulled out a wad of cash so thick that I made a mental note to myself to examine his pants pocket on his way out, to see if the solid wad impacted his profile.

After paying for the bracelets, he asked me again about the Keith Richards project. I nodded, tilted my head, and said "Now why would I do that when I know the shop where you can get it in London, perhaps you'd like the real thing"? Ira shrugged and in his low voice, whispered "I went there. They were incredibly rude to me and made me feel so, well, just Un-cool. Perhaps you could do it and put your spin on it".

"Well, when you put it that way, how can I resist? Not to mention I've been lusting after that bracelet from afar for many years. "It won't be cheap though. I'll do some drawings and we'll take it from there."

Ira half-smiled and for the first time, I noticed how handsome he was. He was in his late 40's and had beautiful, wavy dark hair. He was impeccably groomed with a strong and understated sense of fashion. He had a quiet style that seemed to reflect his shyness and timidity. I liked him but Lizzy scared me a little bit.

Throughout making the Keith Bracelet, Ira and I struck up a friendship. Lizzy was always present. She was bubbly and vibrant, but she annoyed me with the covert control she tried to exert over Ira. Apparently, that's what Ira needed so I tried to like her. I went out to dinner with them because they always knew the best restaurants. They were funny and smart. I was invited to their Tribeca penthouse loft on more than one occasion. It was fabulous on the rooftop with expensive chaise lounges, wooden decking, and elaborate landscaping. The sun poured in through their floor-to-ceiling windows as they pointed out where John F. Kennedy Jr. and Robert DeNiro lived.

I learned that Ira was a garmento and Lizzy was the head designer. He had inherited the 50-year-old family business from his ex-wife's father. He had two teenage boys whom he rarely saw. I sensed a scandal with Lizzy but didn't press it.

He was pretty matter of fact when he told me that his company ripped off other designer's dress designs, manufactured them in-house, and then sold them to the Russian Mob for cash. Lots of cash. But hard times had fallen on the NY Garment Industry and times just weren't what they had been since China had become the cheapest importer of counterfeit design culture. So here we were, inside Ira and Lizzy's loft when he revealed to me that he kept a large trunk of cash at the end of his bed. He couldn't travel because of it. He couldn't go on vacations. He was nervous. I listened as Lizzy told me the stories of emptying various bank safe deposit boxes all over town, dragging heavy suitcases bigger than her. Somewhere between the lines, an IRS agent was investigating their company, and an IRS audit wasn't far behind. When Ira told me about dumping reams of incriminating papers into the Hudson River during the dead of night on several occasions, I felt saddened by what I perceived to be his golden handcuffs.

I thought we were friends when I took Lizzy and Ira to see a decrepit building on a foggy morning in Williamsburg, just underneath the Bridge. The air was so thick with dirt and grime that you almost didn't notice the overflow in the garbage cans outside the Bodega on South Fourth St. I was thinking of buying this building, but I still needed 30K to cover the renovations. I hadn't been able to acquire access to this one-story brick building due to a legal fight between the current tenant and owners, so my realtor and I borrowed an extendable ladder and climbed onto the roof to imagine its interior layout. Buildings in Williamsburg were still cheap, and it didn't escape me that Ira had a trunk full of cash. I blindly put a bid on this building, which was once owned by Dr. Markowitz who was now deceased and who had lived in the back with his offices in the front. It was here that he grew his practice, eventually moved to the suburbs, and continued to service the surrounding Orthodox and Hispanic communities on South Fourth St. I knew Ira was a businessman with deep reserves of "creativity". I asked him for a loan, and he said he'd think about it, nodding yes at the same moment. Lizzy was stony in her silence, and I noticed that her rosebud lips were turned down at the corners in a pout. I'd built my business on repaid personal loans, the hard way: Self-written contracts with money handed under tabletops, what could be any different?

I went forward with the mortgage application. I kept asking Ira for his answer to my loan request and he would reply in jokes and puzzles. Sometimes he would say, "I have to ask Lizzy", which I thought seemed ridiculous. I was too blinded by my wishes and dreams to see how nervous he was. And then he stopped taking my phone calls. The last message I left was the day before the closing of the building sale. My phone call to him was never returned.

Later that evening I had so much anxiety I could barely speak. I was the lead actor in my own drama, and I felt as if I was about to go onstage without any pants. I walked over to my friend Patie's apartment because I had an appointment with her. Pattie is a psychic and a card reader with fiery red hair and ice-blue eyes. Sometimes she's on, sometimes she's off, but she is always direct. I told her my story and started to cry. Without the 30K, I couldn't sign the papers on the building. Patie tilted her head back and laughed a laugh that seemed cruel. She threw her hands down on the table and shouted, "So YOU'RE the one I'm supposed to loan the money to! I just did a reading for myself and that's what came up! I sold my Long Island Home last week and I have the cash I need to invest". The contract, needless to say, was signed the next day.

Years later, I saw Ira and Lizzy trying to avoid me at the Flea Market in Woodstock. I had nothing to say to them, but I had heard that their business had shut down and Lizzy had opened a store in

Tribeca where she was designing and making her clothing designs. It was the University of Life that taught me to beware of hidden agendas, mine included.

"Keith Richard" Bracelet, my version, 1993

[13] Copyright and Infringement

I was keenly aware of my personal style and tenacity for engineering. Locks and clasps were my fascination and forte. After my experience at Artwear, I was forced to come to terms with the concept of "originality". What was original? Was anything original? Did originality even exist? Many times, I would be thinking of a design and then see it in a fashion magazine. Other times, I would be walking down the street doing some window shopping and see it displayed in the window.

I decided to research this and discovered that in the world of fashion and jewelry design it was very difficult to prove. The change of one minute detail in a design could not deem the design original and it was not enough for legal copyright infringement. Plus, copyrighting every design was expensive. I decided that nothing was original, and everything had been done before. I developed a protocol of documenting and dating my designs in my sketchbooks, and I photographed my work diligently.

I programmed my salespeople to look at the credit cards they received for payment. I instructed them to keep a copy of the order receipts and credit card receipts in a file folder under the counter if they suspected anything peculiar.

This proved to be beneficial when a client called me at the store one day. "Barbara, have you sold your work to Macy's? I could swear that I saw your pirate hoops in the jewelry department there." Horrified, I jumped on the subway and went to the jewelry department at Macy's to see for myself.

I had designed this specific line of earring hoops when Hal Rubenstein had said to me, "Barbara, why don't you design hoop earrings for men?" I researched hoop earrings and discovered that pirates wore their gold hoops to finance their funerals: The larger the gold hoop, the bigger the funeral! I had hated hoop earrings because they always looked the same to me and they were such a staple in everyday earring wear, I found them boring and useless. The pirate legend gave me a new appreciation for the common hoop earring. What I failed to see was how much I hated changing out my personal jewelry. Never having been a person who likes to change out their jewelry or even take it off when I sleep, I realized I could do something completely different. I also hated post earrings that stabbed me in the back of my ear when I slept or talked on the phone. I thought about this endlessly until I developed a way to have a hinged mechanism that would lock down the ear wire and clasp it down. The locking mechanism was not visible when the earring was worn, and it was endlessly comfortable. These "lock down" earrings became a staple for my line, but they are very common now.

Sure enough, I saw my 3-ball hoops, plain and symbol pirate earrings displayed on the Macy's silver counter. They had simply cut off the ear wire mechanism (which is very laborious) and replaced it with a post and clutch. I was shocked and deflated but imagine my surprise when I ran back to my store and in the files under the counter found a receipt for these earrings purchased by an executive at Macy's with a federated store credit card a year prior. I had them! (or so I thought!)

I found a copyright lawyer in Soho and had an extensive education in copyright infringement within the walls of her office. Because I had not copyrighted these designs, I was not eligible for damages, but I could sue for legal fees and get Macy's to cease and desist. Ultimately, my legal fees were covered, and they stopped manufacturing the earrings. The attorney also helped me copyright some locks/clasps I had developed. Curiously, she said she had to submit these copyrights as equestrian hardware which I found odd. This is when I realized that believing in my own originality was good, but having legal advice was a necessity.

"Pirate Hoops", 1986, Copyright infringement, Macy's

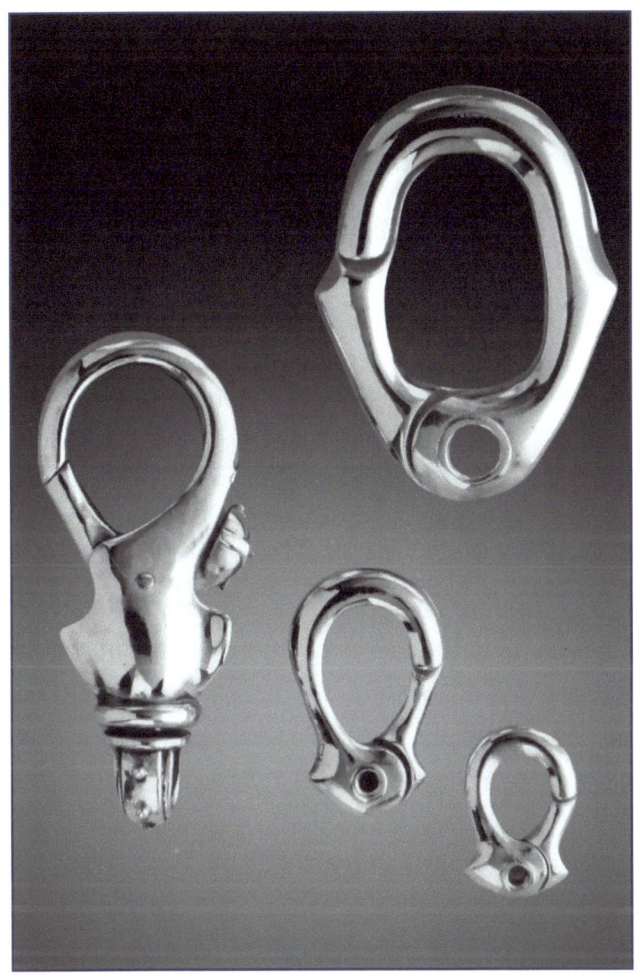

BK Lobster Locks and Swivel Lock, copyright, 1998

[14] Leaving NYC

When the stock market fell in 1998, my business on Thompson St. had completely changed and my patrons who strolled by my store on their walk to Wall Street with wads of cash in their pockets had all but disappeared. The wholesale market had dried up for me because other stores were returning unsold merchandise and trying to negotiate lower prices for new orders. Wholesale hardly seemed worth it when I wasn't receiving full retail pricing. Making multiple items and being more of a manufacturer than an artist didn't move me to create.

I was exhausted emotionally and physically from running the store, managing 7 employees, and overseeing my wholesale/retail business. I missed nature and I needed revitalization. On January 31st, 1999, my partner and I were walking our dogs around McCarren Park in Williamsburg, when we found a small plastic, green pine tree at our feet. We picked it up and since I'm such a fan of tiny things, we placed it on the dashboard of our burgundy Ford Taurus beater. We drove around with that little pine tree on our dashboard for over a year.

When we decided to sell the Williamsburg building and close the store, it was no easy decision. I remember attending a social function with a very high-profile jewelry editor and as we were leaving and saying our goodbyes, I told her of my plans. She said to me, "Call me when you start making jewelry again". I thought to myself, "Is she being snide? I'll never stop making jewelry!" At the time, I had no idea how difficult it would be to reinvent myself heading into middle age.

I traded my city life for country life on June 7th, 2001. I was so elated to leave NYC that I jumped from the cab of the moving truck, got down on my hands and knees and kissed the ground. 3 months later while doing renovations to the new house on 10 acres (with a Christmas Tree farm!), we all watched in horror as the Twin Towers fell on 9/11. My store on Thompson St. had looked upon these towers for years and I could not imagine the devastation that had enveloped that area. If I had stayed, we would have had to close the shop and I would not have been eligible for insurance reimbursement because I conducted so much of my business off the books. I had dodged a bullet, but the world had not. I was stunned and heartbroken.

I set up a new studio and hired several employees as I expanded my wholesale business. Sundance catalog had become a good resource for my earrings, but they paid Net 60 which meant I had to pay all the labor and materials on a Net 30 basis. If I needed the money sooner than Net 60, Sundance would take a 2% discount on the cost of the wholesale order. I had quite a run with my earrings in Sundance Catalog until I discovered that they had started reproducing them under their own label overseas. I sent them a letter and then they dropped me.

After my business with Sundance dried up, I started designing for other designers and businesses. These designs were freelance work, and all done by hand. Designing collections had always been easy for me and I loved this kind of work. I thought I had reached the pinnacle of my career when a very large Italian house commissioned designs for the hardware on their handbags. There was talk of a visit to their Italian studio and factories. They liked my designs until they pressed me to move forward and sign a contract. At the time, my wholesale orders had been secured by a large NYC design repping house. I sought their advice and researched what I should have the contract say. I asked for a percentage of sales and use of my name in the products I would design for them. A dear friend had orchestrated the collaboration initially and he was now saying repeatedly that they would never "go for it". Well, I thought, we must start somewhere, and someone once told me, "Start at the top and negotiate down". I thought they would come back with a counteroffer. Instead, I was ghosted as my friend and the colleagues at my repping house wouldn't return my phone calls. I had shot too high. I cried for a year at the end of this deal and realized how fickle the world of fashion is.

After hand-drawn design, computer assisted design became the core of all jewelry design jobs. If I didn't know CAD, freelance design work was out of the question. I researched learning CAD because I love computers but that meant I would spend less time at the bench which was my daily salvation. Working with my hands and making something kept my anxiety at bay. The learning curve for CAD was 1-2 years and it was evident to me that my knowledge of technical processes in the art of jewelry making would help in the process. However, I was far into middle age at this point, and taking the time and energy to learn CAD would not only keep me from my bench work but waste the time I did have left to live and create from my heart. Who knows how long my hands and eyesight would hold out? Ultimately, I realized I could always hire someone freelance to do CAD for me and have done so since.

I began doing Craft Shows but I soon discovered that this was a new endeavor completely. I originally liked the idea of having the freedom to work in blocks of time in my studio and then traveling to a show for several days of retail and communion with the public. I still do this seasonally, but I have reduced the number of shows I do yearly because traveling and setting up/tearing down is physically challenging and emotionally draining for me. I prefer the peace of my studio with time to daydream. With the invention of the internet, it has brought connection with clients all over the world and now communication is viable in the middle of the woods.

[15] What Cancer Brought Me

In 2002 I remember sitting in my doctor's office and hearing her say, "Prepare to be tortured for two years". "Really?", I thought to myself, "two years"? How was I to make money during surgery, chemo, and radiation? I had just moved to upstate NY from NYC and had little to no friends in my new environment. Plus, my 15-year relationship with Rebeca had just ended when she left me during my chemo treatments. My sister and I had been estranged for 20 years and we had recently reconnected. We were calling each other in July of 2002 saying, "I think I have lung cancer" and "I think I have breast cancer." She was gone by December, and we never got to say Goodbye. In addition, I had a 10-acre Christmas Tree Farm to maintain and eight animals to nurture.

While I sat bloated and panicked from the chemo, I pondered my future. I tried to hire people and continue my relationship with Sundance catalog doing wholesale orders they placed in dramatic dozens until I found they had taken my earring design and subcontracted them to be made overseas. I hated doing multiples of anything that resembled mass production. I turned to teaching classes in my studio which I thoroughly enjoyed but between the cancer treatments and taking care of a large house and property my energy level lagged and my enthusiasm waned.

Eventually, I borrowed money from my father which got me through six months of my new reality. I started working on my "acts of art" which were acts of my love. Things that brought me joy on my spiritual journey.

I had watched three close girlfriends die of breast cancer at a very young age just when they were at the height of their creativity. I was sure I was going to die, and I questioned what this was all about: the struggle, the pain, the suffering. Where was the joy? I feel like I had to consciously consider whether I wanted to live or die because it was so bleak and sad for me at that time. I decided I wasn't done, so I chose life and let go of the small stuff that was weighing me down. I let go of control and ambition.

All through my life, I had collected things that I thought I would "make something with someday". I had found a miniature hand-painted porcelain portrait in an antique store in Adamstown, PA in 1994. At the time, I could barely afford it, but I bought it and tucked it away in a velveteen pouch in one of the drawers in my workbench.

Looking through my drawers and boxes one sad day, I pulled out the small hand-painted porcelain piece that had the portrait of a monk or a priest, complete with a halo. Young and handsome, he was holding a cross and gazing into it, with a crown sitting on his table below. It seemed to me that he was silently asking the same questions I was harboring. I held this porcelain and it felt cool on my palm. It felt magical and inspirational. I imagined that it was delicately painted by someone long ago in a faraway place, but its journey was not yet complete. Over the years I'd take it out every so often to touch its smooth surface and marvel. That's when I decided to call him "The Seeker", someone who was just like me: seeking to learn and to find my answers. Someone like me, someone like everyone. I loved his faint, golden halo and his quest for devotion looking down upon the crown on the table. I developed a sense of comfort every time I gazed upon the upturned corners of his lips, a slight smile in the calm of his acceptance.

When I first studied the art of jewelry, I became fascinated by the work of Faberge I'd seen at the Cleveland Museum of Art. I appreciated the craftsmanship and folly of the famous eggs made in his studio. I longed to hold one in my hands and discover its mystery as I'd peel it open like an intricately wrapped gift. What an incredible experience it must have been for the Russian Tsars to have received such a masterpiece from the studios of Faberge. I imagined these artifacts resting on a marble mantelpiece or an elaborately carved desk, waiting to be touched and discovered like a magical toy. But I would want to WEAR it and keep it with me always.

It took me almost two years to complete this portraiture locket. It kept getting increasingly complicated by my obsession with hardware and locking mechanisms. This became an act of love with my devotion to love and beauty. It opens, it closes, it locks. The porcelain can be removed from the setting. The pearls on the outside of the "ring of fire" are pearls of wisdom. There is a gold halo because I'm earning mine. There is a hollow ear because we must listen. There are 3 golden tears with rubies because each tear we shed has an inner lesson. It is meant to be worn, hung on the wall, or sitting on a desk, waiting to be explored and opened like the flower that blooms in the truth we seek.

New Information about "The Seeker" (months later..)

> After publishing this blog post about "The Seeker", a dear client took it upon herself to research the image in the vintage porcelain. Thank you, Jane Wood, for your keen detective work!
>
> *Aloysius Gonzag: Born in the castle of Castigione, 1568; died, in June 1591.

The eldest of 7 children in a wealthy family in Northern Italy, he was chosen to be trained in the military but received "the calling" to be a priest at a very young age. His family was vehemently opposed to this but when he developed persistent health issues, he was sent to a monastery and furthered his education there. In 1591, a plague broke out in Rome and the Jesuits opened a hospital for the stricken. Aloysius volunteered to work there. Six days before his 23rd Birthday, Aloysius showed the first symptoms of being infected. He recovered, but his health was left worse than ever. He had a vision that he would be dead within the year and told several people that he would die on the Octave of the feast of Corpus Christie. On that very day, he seemed well in the morning but insisted he would die before the day was over. He died just before midnight.

Owing to the manner of his death, he has always been considered a patron saint of plague victims. For his compassion and courage in the face of an incurable disease, Alysius Gonzaga has become the patron both of AIDS sufferers and their caretakers. Aloysius is the patron saint of Valmontone, a town not far from Rome.

In Art, St. Aloysius is shown as a young man wearing a black cassock and surplice, or as a page. His attributes are a lily, referring to innocence; a cross, referring to piety and sacrifice; a skull, referring to his early death; and a rosary, referring to his devotion.

It is curious to me that this little porcelain was crafted by me, unknowingly into something of a shrine to the testament of knowledge and healing. I, too, feel like I live in an age of many plagues. I have seen many profound and talented souls die of AIDS, cancer, and now covid. We seek to heal.

Saint Aloysius-Gonzaga Portrait

My reliquary "The Seeker",
2014, Sterling Silver, Gold, Pearls, Rubies,
Vintage hand-painted porcelain, Fabricated

[16] Living to Create

"Working in Relative Obscurity"

This was a Beautiful Day, a day when almost anything seemed possible. We are broken but we will "pick ourselves up and dust ourselves off" (to quote the new president, Barack Obama). The heavens, can you hear us? I was not the only one with tears streaming down my face, tears of joy and hope, perhaps a reason to carry on.

And speaking of picking myself up and dusting myself off, it is something I've been doing for years when I had no understanding of the process or the meaning. The Today Show defined it that morning when they were interviewing Isabel Toledo, an artist and designer who "has worked in relative obscurity for over 25 years". She is the clothing designer who designed the beautiful "lemongrass yellow" ensemble Michelle Obama wore to her husband's inauguration. I had heard of her work for years and followed her trajectory peripherally. In my world, she was not obscure, but I guess that was relative.

"Relative Obscurity" is a term I'd never considered. It brought to mind a gentleman I met in 1996. His name was Huesti. He was old in 1996, perhaps close to 85. He was a retired railroad mechanic in New Hampshire whom I'd been privileged to meet through a fellow metalsmith. My friend was having something made by Huesti that would fit into the clock that he had been commissioned to repair for a private yacht club. We visited Huesti in the fall while the colorful leaves were falling on the little house where he lived with his wife, Gracie. Upon entering I noticed how small and unassuming Huesti was. As I glanced around the house, I noticed that the first and second floors were filled with clocks: back to back clocks were stacked on top of each other, piles of clocks. There was minimal furniture, only grandfather clocks, wall clocks, and mantel clocks. I was overwhelmed with the collective ticking and chiming as all the clocks struck noon. All the clocks were set in tandem and chimed like a Cathedral on Sunday morning. He liked to repair clocks.

Huesti shuffled and ushered us down the narrow stairs to his basement workshop. We could hardly walk but for a small passageway that wove itself between lathes, vertical drilling machines, milling machines, and other large equipment. I looked up and saw that there was a miniature train track suspended from the ceiling just above eye level. I had to duck my head around the tracks as I gathered my jacket tightly around my body to avoid snagging it on all the tightly packed machinery into this small basement workspace. I saw model trains that were designed and created to scale in stainless steel, silver, nickel, and brass. They were magnificent. Each one was beautifully crafted with tiny brass and stainless-steel ornamentation. They traveled and hummed around the suspended miniature rails flashing with speed and sparkle. On his small workbench was a rail car in the process of construction. Tiny screws and gears were spread out on a small bit of muslin fabric awaiting assembly. Metal shavings were swept into a small pile at the corner of his workbench. I imagined Huesti in his magnifying glasses as he worked silently in his magical place that was invisible to the eyes of the world.

That day I could hardly speak as my friend and I walked down the stone walkway towards the car. Huesti was brilliant and I will never forget this talent who worked in "relative obscurity". I have always felt simpatico with Huesti, reminding myself that there are millions of talents in this world and across America who work tirelessly, without fame or recognition, merely for the passion they experience in what they create. That day I realized that I also work in relative obscurity, fueled by the passion for the art that I create. My hands are my Zen and that is enough. Now I do not wait for the fame or the fortune, merely I wait for the sun to rise for the next day in which I can create, imagine, and transform. Truly this is the definition of opportunity.

The Repair Café, May 2018

The wild turkeys roam and call out to me through the sun streaming upon my workbench. It is quiet. It is serene and I have time to contemplate. This is right for me at this time in my life. I am no longer pulled by my dreams that wilt in daylight.

Am I lonely? No, because I have contact: Just the right amount of contact that I choose and which I value. I feel such gratitude now when I sit eating a sandwich at the local diner and watch the old man next to me sitting alone and staring at his gold watch. He looks peaceful. I can see that he's lived a full life.

I love him silently and admire him. What were his choices and where did he stumble or astound?

My life is much smaller than it used to be, and I like it that way. I moved to my cottage in the woods almost two years ago and it's taken me that long to find the moonlight on the path when it's dusk. It's taken me that long to reach out and wander the perimeters of my town. That's when I found the Repair Café.

The Repair Café is an old concept. It happens in many incarnations in many communities. I remember when I was a child how I sat by my father's elbow and watched him closely when he fixed a broken chair or metal shelving. When he drilled through the metal and attached nuts and bolts for stability it seemed almost painful, like a stay in the hospital. The drill through the metal screamed when it was mended. It sighed as it was sanded and repainted. We laughed when he was stumped by an engineering challenge, and we wondered why the piece didn't repair itself.

I've been making jewelry for 45 years and I like to take my time. I volunteered my time one-afternoon several years ago at the Woodstock Repair Café. I was there to advise and do small jewelry repairs on the spot in a large room at the back of a church. Volunteers were buzzing around, setting up tables and lamps. I worked a double task of sewing and mending as well as wielding my pliers to fix that broken clasp on a long chain.

The Café had barely opened its doors when a couple of real Woodstockers walked up to my small jewelry station. He was dapper and friendly. She was tall and monumental in her fuscia fake fur coat and purple hair. They were clutching a round cookie tin.

Putting the tin down, they slid it over the table to me and I opened it. Resting in a square of red velvet was a silver and semi-precious stone pendant, one of the largest pendants I'd ever seen. Immediately I knew it was modernist, from the 1950s when many artists also made jewelry. It resembled a Paul Klee painting with fanciful and playful beaded silver wires sticking out randomly. It was odd and intriguing and a little bit garish.

"Can you fix this?" she asked. "It's quite valuable, by an artist that used to live here in Woodstock: Rolph Scarlett."

I examined the big pendant and saw that it needed a solder job because one of the jump rings on the main, hollow form had snapped. Soldering a piece of jewelry is always a challenge when someone else has made the piece. Not to mention the care that is needed to preserve the original patina. Turning it over in my hands I could see that while it was somewhat primitive, it had been made with intention and humor. I liked this odd piece of jewelry and was intrigued by the person who had been Rolph Scarlett.

I could fix it. It would be a challenge and a bit scary, but I knew I could do it. Plus, I love the fantasy that I can be part of a bit of history by carrying on the tradition of artists who work in metal. I carried the piece back to my studio and researched Rolph Scarlett.

"Scarlett was Canadian-born, came of age in the Midwest, and spent a few important years in Hollywood, where he designed stage sets. His work from this early period echoes Klee's use of color, his confidence in naïve, primitive forms, and his blend of abstraction and figuration. In its flat spatial qualities, it prefigures the Indian Space painting of the 1940s by a decade. He moved to New York in 1933 and eventually found his first great patron at the Museum of Non-Objective Painting, directed by Baroness Hilla Rebay and art patron Solomon R. Guggenheim. Guggenheim would collect over 60 works by Scarlett for his collection, more than any other artist outside of Vasily, Kandinsky and Rudolf Bauer."

It turns out that Scarlett was friends with Paul Klee and admired his work greatly. Scarlett's paintings are beautiful and similar, but he never really gained world recognition like Klee. He lost the support of patrons when his style changed and he retired to Woodstock where he lived in "regional obscurity" to the end of his life, returning to his original passion of making jewelry.

This week on a quiet day in the studio I said a silent prayer while I soldered the pendant. I had taken it apart to repair it. The patina changed when the piece was heated but I re-oxidized it back to its aged splendor. I reassembled the pieces and imagined Rolph stamping the piece with his preordained nod to street graffiti. Rolph and I shared that fascination and I still incorporate graffiti images into my work.

The pendant needed a "bale" from which it could hang on a chain. I chose one of my "beaded bales" that are a signature staple of my design collections. I thought about this choice. I knew that ethically I should choose a plain large silver oval jump ring in keeping with Rolph's intention, but I just couldn't do it. On the inside of the bale is my triangle signature.

When I'm old and sitting in a diner, eating my sandwich, and staring at my watch, I will hold the wish that in the future someone might discover a piece of my jewelry and bring it to a Repair Cafe. I hope my signature will be recognized. If another jeweler repairs my work and adds their moniker, it will continue upon its journey. I will know that despite my choice of relative and regional obscurity as a career path, I'd made a mark on the path well-traveled.

"YOU'RE SO TALENTED"

[17] The Journey of the Balangandan Necklace

During the COVID-19 lockdown, I was talking with a fellow jewelry designer, and she began telling me about an amazing piece of history, the Balangandan Necklace. The Balangandan originated in the 17th century and was worn generally in the 18th and 19th centuries by Brazilian women of African descent. It can be worn at the waist, as a necklace, a bracelet, an amulet, or used as a door hanging. The Balangandan are primarily made of copper, gold, or silver, with hanging charms that are meaningful in the wearer's life. Some charms are spiritual, representing African Orishas or Christian deities. Others are meant to impart good fortune or to commemorate important life events. As I began researching the Balangandan, I found images and was struck by the pride and power of these women. I'm not sure if they were enslaved. Had they been born in Africa? Did they have children or husbands? What were their lives like, what were their hopes and dreams? Had they been transported 3000 miles against their will, never to see home and family again? That very prospect sent chills up my spine and I spent the evening looking out the back window of my house at the trees and starlight and COVID darkness. I held the Mother of Pearl Charm that I'd purchased 25 years ago at a flea market in my hand. I'm not sure of its age or origin, but it's always felt like a transformational piece for me. And at that moment I was inspired to begin work on a Balangandan of my own as a tribute to slavery and women everywhere. I've always been intrigued by charms, their beauty, and

BK Balangandan Necklace, 2020

their meaning. I wondered at passages and changes in my own life and the significant things, both physical and emotional that I've accumulated over the years.

I created my 2020 version of a Balangandan to exemplify an eternal reverence for the hopes and dreams of women everywhere. I built the piece around the central Mother of Pearl charm and made the chain links to represent barbed wire, the horrors of chattel slavery, and the extraordinary perseverance and strength of the women who survived. I chose opals and moonstones to honor hopes and dreams: the things we wish for and the reality of our everyday lives. I adorned the corners of the silver plate with Aladdin's lamps to inspire magic.

All the charms represent a woman's journey: children, growth and daily tasks, emotional and physical strength, love, and loss on a life's path well-traveled. Some of the charms are vintage and some of them I made. Each charm has a meaning to the concept of the piece.

The Balangandan can be worn on the neck or at the waist. It can also hang on a wall by the front door, as it often did in 19th-century Brazil. I intend that the owner add their personal charms to commemorate their individual soul's journey.

The Charms on my Balangandan Necklace:

I mimicked the original shape of the silver plate from which the charms hang to give reference to the ships in which the enslaved Africans traveled to the New World. This shape, to me, also represents the sea of life and the Orisha Yemaya. The opals and moonstones represent the dreams we hold as individuals on our journey. The Aladdin's Lamps on either side of the holder represent spirits that watch over us as well as listen to our hopes and dreams.

"YOU'RE SO TALENTED"

Above: (Left) Vintage Photo of slave wearing their Balangandan
(Right) Man Ray's wife, Juliet, photographed by him wearing a Balangandan Necklace

Mother of Pearl charm & Lense Charm

Top Row: (left to right)

1.) The articulated mermaid. Vintage Silver Charm. Because I always wanted to see, if not be, a mermaid.
2.) Vintage Silver Chalet charm. We all deserve the home of our dreams.
3.) Motorcycle Boot. To kick some ass when we need to.
4.) Baby Shoe. The hope of a new life and rebirth.
5.) Vintage dice charm. Silver and Acrylic. Because sometimes a little luck is involved.
6.) Vintage silver pickaxe. Because sometimes you have to keep chipping away on something until it gives way.
7.) Vintage Silver Hope Chest. Because we collect things and store them in our hearts.
8.) My wisdom tooth from bone loss. Silver. One of the things I've lost along my journey.

Bottom Row: (left to right)

1.) Vintage Sewing scissors in a leather worn sheath. Because there are things we need to mend or cut out of our lives. An ode to the chatelaine.
2.) Silver Chicken Foot Charm. A nod to Santeria, religious beliefs, and magic.
3.) Vintage lenses holding a silver screen with which I've embroidered a cracked heart. Because sometimes our hearts break and retain a crack.
4.) Vintage Mother Of Pearl Charm. (see above) Each "card" seems to represent the major arcana of a tarot deck. This charm was probably originally used as a divining tool.
5.) Vintage Silver and Mother or Pearl Baby Rattle. Because sometimes we need to entertain and distract our children, or even ourselves.
6.) Vintage Silver Knight in Shining Amor. Because we all want to be saved or find "the one"
7.) "Under the Sea" Vintage Painting on glass set in Silver. Because I have dreams of a city under the sea where I can live peacefully.
8.) Vintage carved wooden Shoe Charm. Because everyone needs to walk a mile in another person's shoes.

"YOU'RE SO TALENTED"

BK Balangandan modeled by Maria. Photo by Amanda Rubin.

THE JOURNEY OF THE BALANGANDAN NECKLACE

* * * * * *

Afro-brazilian Amulet
March, 2016
From the Museum of Ethnology,

As the indigenous peoples who worked on the Portuguese colonial plantations in Brazil died out or fled, they were replaced by African slaves, who brought with them elements of their home cultures. The African territories they came from, a number which boasted fairly advanced metallurgical industries.

The balangandan is a religious object typical of Brazil, and particularly of the state of Bahia, that represents the encounter between African and European cultures. In Portuguese, it is called a penca, or bouquet, while the name balangandan is an onomatopoetic word meant to recall the sound made by the object's dangling metal baubles.

Consisting of a number of charms strung on a common fastener hung from a chain, the balangandan traces its roots back to the 17th century, though its more general use dates to the 18th-19th centuries. Worn by women of African descent, the balangandan most frequently adorned the thick chain belts that hung about slaves' waists, though on special occasions, it might be attached to the wrist. When not in use, it hung in the house near the door. Originally made of silver, the balangandan represented significant monetary value and was not infrequently presented by plantation owners to favored slaves. Each balangandan was unique, having been composed to reflect the specific life path of its wearer. Its charms included religious symbols that could be interpreted simultaneously as Christian in origin, or as representing certain African gods. Other charms were intended to impart good fortune, happiness, prosperity, or good health, while a third type was selected out of gratitude for - and in commemoration of - having survived some misfortune, such as an accident or illness. The function of the balangandan was in some respects like that of a modern charm bracelet.

The charms of the balangandan frequently depicted plants or fruits such as the pomegranate, symbolizing wealth or fertility. One common motif was that of the gourd vessel or dipper, which several African cultures used as a symbol for the female womb. Another was that of a hand posed in what is known as the 'fig' gesture, or figa, with the thumb protruding from between the curled index and middle fingers. Originally a Mediterranean symbol used to impart fertility and ward off evil spirits, the figa is still a very popular symbol in Brazil today. The fastener on which the charms were strung was representative of the ships that brought the slaves to the New World, the birds that sat on either side symbolizing the continents of Africa and the Americas.

Post Balangandan: An Act of Art becomes an Act of Misappropriation:

In November of 2020, I was spending another weekend with my pod in a beautiful and healing upstate sanctuary. There were four of us and I had brought my completed Balangandan Necklace to show them. One of the women whom I had met there previously was becoming a close friend and she was a well-connected NYC jewelry designer, younger than me. I will call her Sabi and she is of Hindi descent. Sabi was smart, funny, generous, and talented. She is a gemologist with the finest collection of jewels she sells out of her office in Midtown, NY. Sabi is a jewelry designer as well and we often joked about our experiences and the difficulties of working with "Old School" male jewelers when we needed stone setters or fabricators as subcontractors. As women makers, we shared the challenges of not being taken seriously throughout our careers.

Since moving from NYC to the Hudson Valley in 2000, I had stepped away from my world of industry connections and made my living and my work outside of that system by choice.

When I pulled my Balangandan out of its covered tray, Sabi gasped in shock and clapped her hands to her cheeks. "This is magnificent, Barbara", she said. "This is museum-worthy and I think I know some museum directors whose contacts I can share with you." I was overcome with gratitude and joy. That weekend my friend Amanda offered to do some model shots with the necklace and Sabi offered to model. The photos were gorgeous. She posed with the large piece around her waist and her neck. She looked beautiful in her white dress and dark skin. As a woman of color, I thought the photos were relevant to the history of the Balangandan and I couldn't have asked for a better model.

Concurrently, Sabi was in conversation with the two women producers of Jewelry Week in NYC. Sabi thought my work and my history exemplifying the tradition of female metalsmiths in the '80s might be an interesting story to tell, along with the Balanganden within the social environment of "Black Lives Matter". Sabi helped me write the proposal, choose the photographs, and facilitated the introduction to the producers. At this time, we did not know the theme of the upcoming NYC jewelry week.

Finally, a virtual interview was held with the show organizers. I had set up my Balangandan Necklace on my velvet mannequin behind me in my studio and chosen a few of my favorite recent pieces to show the producers. During the interview, my efforts to show them and talk about the Balangandan were met with blank faces and disinterested stares. When I tried to explain my journey in making the piece and its importance in cultural history that related to slavery, oppression, and all women, their eyes looked elsewhere, and they changed the subject. I tried to speak about my days in the '80s when I lived and worked in my store on 7th Street and had my first break at Artwear. "Are you still in contact with Robert Lee Morris"? they asked? I felt my heart sink and answered a meek "yes" because I had had an interesting and painful experience with Robert during my tenure at his gallery.

"Perhaps you both could arrange a talk together," they said. That was the last thing I wanted to do. "Or perhaps you could arrange to teach a short class online virtually" during our event. This did not interest me, and it even felt a little insulting. These two women were young, hadn't been artists through the '80s, 90's and 2000's, yet they were the product of our forebearers before them, paving the way for women creators in jewelry. After the virtual interview, I became sad and withdrawn.

Weeks later, at another lovely weekend with my pod at the sanctuary, Sabi was there and avoided my direct gaze all weekend. She had asked me to bring the Balangandan that weekend so we could do our own interview. I brought my tripod and camera, which sat in the back of my car silently. She never suggested the interview and feeling shunned and silenced by the NYC Jewelry Week producers, I didn't mention it. Finally, we were all sitting in the sunroom a few minutes prior to leaving and Amanda said to me, "Barbara, since you posted the piece on your blog, what has been the reaction?". Sabi looked down into her glass of water between her hands, resting on her lap. "Well,", I said, "it's been pretty positive. One person even wrote 'Queen' under the vintage photo of a slave holding her Balangandan".

Sabi looked up at Amanda and said, "Well, I've had some pushback about the piece since I posted the picture you took of me wearing it on my Instagram page. Two colleagues who are very well connected in the museum & library world called me and said it was 'all kinds of wrong'. No museum would EVER buy this piece for their collections. I could hear the sadness in their voices. They were women of color raising bi-racial children and they thought it inappropriate and disrespectful."

I was stunned. I could feel my heart starting to pound inside my chest. It had been several weeks since Sabi had posted the photo and she had never mentioned a word to me. Amanda looked at Sabi and said, "Why didn't you call Barbara?"

Later, when we were talking privately about that exchange, Amanda said to me: "I mean if your apartment building was on fire, wouldn't you knock on the door and tell your neighbors?"

Several days later, I attempted to call Sabi and discuss with her the event and exactly what had happened and what she thought. Sabi was too busy and essentially didn't return the phone call for 6 weeks. When we finally did speak, it was apparent that we had very different views on appropriation, and she basically said that I was trying to explain why I was "not a racist".

This experience sent me down the path of discovery and research. Was I a racist? Perhaps that is what the NYC Jewelry Week producers thought of this piece and why I wasn't invited to share at the event. When NYC Jewelry Week did happen virtually in 2020, it was clear to me why my proposal hadn't been chosen: NYCJW was about black voices and my piece, created by a white woman, was too hot a topic and too controversial.

Three months later, Sabi called me to ask me to take down the beautiful photo of her on my blog, which I did. I haven't spoken to her since, and I still miss the friendship. Trust is a difficult thing when one feels betrayed.

Ultimately, I felt it was an incredible journey and a necessary experience. I had to reach out and talk to as many people as I could to find out whether I had spent three months making a piece that was "all kinds of wrong". I researched and talked with friends (black and white) about the Whitney's showing of Dana Schutz's painting of Emmitt Till and the controversy that entailed. I read countless articles about misappropriation in the era of Black Lives Matter.

For me, the most helpful piece of writing came from Brian Morton in Dissent Magazine in the Fall of 2020: "All Shook Up: The Politics of Cultural Appropriation.

After I read the article, it was the first time I breathed a sigh of relief and felt some healing. I reached out to Brian and sent him this letter:

Dear Brian Morton:

I cannot thank you enough for writing this piece. I am a 66-year-old artist and have been struggling with a piece I made and its "misappropriation" in the wake of "Black Lives Matter". As a studio jeweler, I have been making jewelry that supports me as an artist since 1984. However, my passions are the pieces I create in relative obscurity. These are creations that feed my soul and blend humanity. As you so eloquently say: "There are no two people on the planet who don't share a few lanes. The point is that artists imagine the experiences of others by virtue of a common humanity". When I read that line, I took a deep, heavy sigh.

My intention with making these art pieces is to one day have a show, a culmination of my life's work. When I showed my "Balangandan" Necklace to a friend, she posted it on her Instagram feed and was immediately attacked for its misappropriation. She took the post down. I was stunned by this reaction, and it took me down a deep and explorative rabbit hole.

In everything I've read since, nothing has touched me as deeply as your piece of writing about this subject.

My friend had originally told me that my Balengandan necklace was surely a "museum piece". I, too, imagined it to be a significant piece of my time and hold a place in history as a thread to those who came before me. However, after the Instagram incident, her curator friend, who is black, told her that "no museum would ever purchase this piece". My heart sank. I don't know if this is true or not and quite frankly, I don't care because my heart is also full of empathy and love for those who preceded me. I, too, "imagine the minds of others as a sort of moral necessity".

Sincerely, Barbara Klar

He was kind enough to write me back:

Dear Barbara Klar,
I'm sorry to be so long in responding to your generous email. I'm very glad that you liked my piece in Dissent.

Thank you for the link to your blog. It's such an unfortunate sign of the times that the effort to learn more about another culture, and to pay tribute to it and keep the memory of it alive by incorporating its art into one's own artistic practices, is seen as something blameworthy. I think the Balangandan necklaces are remarkable. To make such special creations must be its own reward.

Thank you again for writing.
Brian

And this is the version I hold onto within my heart. I create "acts of art" from "acts of love". My empathy and love inspire me to respect the long history and journeys of those who came before us and carry it into the future so that we may ALL learn and evolve into a more inclusive way of living.

[18] Why I Make Reliquaries & Memento Mori

"Working in Relative Obscurity"

Within the interim between birth and death there is life. In life, there are things we hold onto as memories and mementos. It's a fact that we're born alone and die alone but I'm fascinated by the objects we hold dear to our hearts, the things and memories we collect to ease the pain and celebrate the joy during our life journey.

I've lived through the Aids Crisis, Cancer crisis, and most recently the Covid Crisis. I am profoundly impacted by death and loss. It has not left me unmarked. Making something as a memorial or a tribute to these losses gives me peace.

What can be more special and tender than a memorial to those we've loved and lost or to the things we've held close to our hearts as a talisman. This is where my "act of art" becomes an "act of the heart". In making these pieces it becomes prescient and relevant in these trying times now more than ever.

Here are a few samples of the reliquaries I've made:

Commission, 2019, "Broken Plate" Pin

"YOU'RE SO TALENTED"

WHY I MAKE RELINQUARIES & MEMENTO MORI

Blue Chintz, by Cherie Banks

Born to Swedish immigrants in 1897, Cecelia Louise Samuelson's life spanned a period marked by tragedy and triumph—from a childhood train accident that nearly severed her legs, to financial ruin after the stock market crash of 1929 and her husband's subsequent struggle with alcoholism (and courageous recovery). Cecelia ran two small businesses to help make ends meet while fighting a recurrent battle with cancer that took both of her breasts, narrowly escaped a devastating house fire in 1968, and lived to see a man walk on the moon. She lost her last battle with cancer in 1972.

Cecelia, my grandmother, was the strongest woman I have ever known. I adored her.

In the early 1920s, Cecelia and Arthur were newlyweds strolling through a quaint New York town when a shop window display of vibrant English transferware dishes caught Cecelia's eye. Wavy-edged square plates in Crown Ducal's "Blue Chintz" pattern featured a bright blue background covered with tropical birds, flowers, branches and foliage. Arthur took note, and secretly returned to the shop to buy the luncheon set for her.

After Cecelia passed away, my mother gave the set to me and I displayed the plates on a wall in my home. When one accidentally fell to the floor my heart shattered, too. I gathered the plate fragments and kept them tucked away in a small box. Recently, I took the box out and held one of the pieces in my hands. Locked in a pattern of subtle crazing crisscrossing the 100-year-old surface—still vibrant with colorful birds and flowers—are the smoky traces of that horrific house fire in 1968. Each lovely, jagged fragment represents my grandmother's essence—beauty and strength, personal tragedy and resilience. Barbara Klar is a dear friend and gifted artist who, with silver and bronze, has captured a precious fragment of

Cecelia's life—an exquisite, sublime testament to a woman of great courage who taught me the meaning of unconditional love.

"Sea Bone", 2014, Rose Wood, carved, Silver, Vintage watch crystal, pearl, gold, watercolor, pencil. Fabricated and Cast (Pendant or wall hanging) Hangs 4.5 inches

With a nod to ancient reliquaries and personal talisman I have attempted to create a totem that pays homage to life of the sea. Having found a small crab claw on the beach long ago, I drew the small "gem" and encased it under a watch crystal and set it with a bezel of gold. I then cast the claw and recreated it in yellow gold, which hangs from the bottom of the piece and is removable and wearable as a small charm. The entire piece can be worn on the body or hung on the wall as a testament to the life of the ocean.

Commission, 2021, "Mason's Baby teeth", Silver, bronze, baby teeth, necklace with removable tooth charm

Proud Mom Blair wearing the "Baby Teeth" Necklace

Book Locket, commission 2019, Silver, hair of the Beloved, plexiglass, note, photo, Fabricated. Made for a client memorializing the passing of her husband, a rare book collector.

"My Buddy" Locket, desk frame, or wall art, 2014, gold, silver, painting, hair-"from the tip of his tail" charm (removable). Made in memorial for a friend's dog, Buddy. (stands 4 inches)

Sal Scarpitta Locket, commissioned by a client in memorial to her artist husband, Sal Scarpitta.
https://en.wikipedia.org/wiki/Salvatore_Scarpitta

Some of Sal Scarpitta's work used as inspiration for the Locket

Made through inspiration of his work. Bronze, Brass, Silver, Wood, Photo, hair of the beloved. Fabricated, 2019 (5 inches by 4.5 inches)

"Nature is my God" Reliquary, 2023
Watercolor, vintage celluloid reliquary box, Silver, Plexiglass, Vintage watch crystal, moonstone. 5 inches tall. Charm is removable for wearing

WHY I MAKE RELINQUARIES & MEMENTO MORI

Removable Bird watercolor charm, silver and Gold. "Nature is my God" reliquary, 2023

[19] Doubt (EPILOGUE)

"Working in Relative Obscurity"

The rejections from shows have been equal to, if not more frequent than, the times I've been told I'm so talented. It never gets easy and is often soul deflating.

Only over time have I learned to ride these waves and not take it personally. As I age, I know that my reluctance to socialize and network has directly affected my sales, but I can't seem to care. I tell people that my ambition has disappeared since turning 70.

I read articles in the NY Times about women artists who've been overlooked their entire careers and get recognition in their 70s, 80s, and 90s or get discovered after their death. I can't imagine anything worse than late-in-life recognition because I love the calm serenity of my semi-retirement. My running joke is that before I die, I'm going to dig a hole in my backyard and bury all my treasures to be dug up at a later date.

I am amused that there is a market for my work on Ebay. I now stamp my one off creations "only 1" and hope their value will increase through time. I'm referred to as an "American Metalsmith" in the descriptions. This gives me a sense of self that all my time has not been wasted. It gives me a small pleasure to know that even though I don't have heirs or family, I've made a small impact in my efforts to add more joy and beauty into this world.

I listen to my female friends who've had disappointments in their art careers despite their best efforts. We've jointly concluded that the only reason to make art is because you HAVE to, and because it brings you joy. Perhaps it even brings us closer to the creator. There is only ZEN in our efforts.

Barbara Klar photographed by Franco Vogt, 2023 in her Woodstock, NY studio

ACKNOWLEDGMENTS

I would like to thank the beautiful members of my pod, the ones who have steered me towards the light when I only saw darkness. This is the village of my people:

To Jim Jarmusch, along with his family, who introduced me to art, design, and antiques. To Gail and Al Barracano who first walked into my 7th St. Store in 1986 and became my mentors and chosen family. Cynthia Sley, who always hears me out, inspires me and shares with me her loving family. To Michele Zalopany, who has always supported my work and hosted my private shows in her remarkable salon. To Charlie Spademan, always the source of information, and a wonderful collaborator with endless bad jokes. To Amanda Rubin who always shared information and support when I saw none. To Murdock McKenzie who was infinitely patient and supportive. To Hal Rubenstein who has always generously shared my work with the press and encouraged to make earrings for men! To Thea Fiore-Bloom who gave me the courage to write. To Abbe Aronson who traded a ring to kickstart this book. To Fae Myenne Ng who made me laugh and who gave me endless encouragement. To Moira Dryer for leaving me endless gifts upon her death as well as inspiration in her life. To Victor Alzamora who found a drill press and installed it for me when I had no money. To Stephen Black for believing in me and supporting my craft with many blessings. To his brother, Randolph Black, for finding that first restaurant sink and installing it in my studio (I've carried that sink with me to every studio since!) To Pattie Canova, who loaned me the $30K to buy that building in Williamsburg at the last moment!

And, finally, to all my beautiful clients who believed in and invested in my work the past 40 years. You have given me a reason to carry on. You now bring me hope for the future as your friends and children come to me for their personal treasures too!

www.ingramcontent.com/pod-product-compliance
Lightning Source LLC
Chambersburg PA
CBHW041630220426
43665CB00001B/10